KALI LINUX FOR BE

A practical Guide to Learn the operating system installation and configuration, including Networks, ethical Hacking and the Main Tools explanation for an easy everyday Use

© copyright 2022 - All rights reserved.

The content contained within this book may not be reproduced, duplicated, or transmitted without direct written permission from the author or the publisher.
Under no circumstances will any blame or legal responsibility be held against the publisher, or author, for any damages, reparation, or monetary loss due to the information contained within this book, either directly or indirectly.
Legal Notice:

This book is copyright protected. It is only for personal use. You cannot amend, distribute, sell, use, quote or paraphrase any part, or the content within this book, without the consent of the author or publisher.
Disclaimer Notice:

please note the information contained within this document is for educational and entertainment purposes only. All effort has been executed to present accurate, up to date, reliable, complete information. No warranties of any kind are declared or implied. Readers acknowledge that the author is not engaging in the rendering of legal, financial, medical, or professional advice. The content within this book has been derived from various sources. please consult a licensed professional before attempting any techniques outlined in this book.
By reading this document, the reader agrees that under no circumstances is the author responsible for any losses, direct or indirect, that are incurred as a result of the use of information contained within this document, including, but not limited to, errors, omissions, or inaccuracies.

contents

chapter one: Introduction to Linux

chapter Two- Linux everyday

chapter Three - Installing Linux

chapter Four-An Introduction to Kali Linux

chapter Five- Making Kali a USB Bootable Device

chapter Six – The most popular Kali Linux tools

chapter Seven- Basics of Networking

chapter eight- proxy and proxy chains

chapter Nine- Virtual private Networks

chapter Ten- Installing VpN on Kali Linux

Installing VpN on Kali Linux

chapter eleven- Securing and monitoring Kali Linux

chapter Twelve- Debian package Management

chapter Thirteen- Advanced Usage

chapter one: Introduction to Linux

everything present on the planet works under a specific order. Nature involving people, creatures, plants, seasons, climate, and so on, have a specific way wherein they work. The least demanding guide to consider is of people who are talented with a mind to think. This cerebrum goes about as the operating system when Human operating System involving the digestive system, respiratory system, administrative system, and so forth, are considered. Similarly, when we talk about innovation, we talk about the advancement of innovation. Many decades have cruised by, and the quickest developing field on the planet is the field of Information Technology.

each innovation somehow or another or different has an operating system liable for controlling and dealing with the individual gadget's tasks. For example, on the off chance that we take a gander at the case of a desktop computer, we definitely realize it has an operating system installed to it. Throughout the years, there have been a few operating systems made for such reason at the same time, few out of every have demonstrated to be compelling.

Let us start with first understanding the need and reason for an operating system.

each time you switch on your pc, you see a screen where you can perform various exercises like compose, peruse the web or watch a video. Would it be that makes the pc equipment work that way? How does the processor on your pc realize that you are requesting that it run an mp3 record?

Indeed, it is the operating system or the portion which does this work. A piece is a program at the core of any operating system that deals with essential stuff, such as letting equipment speak with programming.

In this way, to chip away at your pc, you need an operating System (oS). presently, you may have utilized famous oS resembles Windows, Apple oS X however here we will realize what Linux is and what benefits it offers over different oS decisions.

In the present express, the most generally utilized operating system for personal computers is Windows oS and Apple oS be that as it may; the hisToRy goes back to a few dissemination and renditions of operating systems at any point made. The most popular and open source of all is Linux.

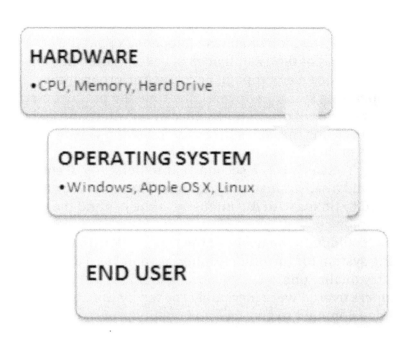

Figure 1. operating System working as an intermediate between hardware and software.

The historical backdrop of Linux started in 1991, when the savage desolation of the virus war was bit by bit reaching a conclusion. There was a demeanour of harmony and quietness that won in the skyline. In the field of registering, an extraordinary future appeared to be in the offing, as amazing equipment pushed the breaking points of the pcs past what anybody anticipated. In any case, there was all the while something missing and it was none other than the operating Systems, where an incredible void appeared to have showed up.

For a certain something, DoS was all the while ruling in its immense realm of pcs. purchased by Bill Gates from a Seattle programmer for $50,000, the stripped down operating system had sneaked into each side of the world by ethical means of a sharp advertising methodology. pc clients had no other decision. Apple Macs were better, yet with cosmic costs that no one could bear, they stayed a skyline away from the enthusiastic millions.

The other committed camp of figuring was the UNIX world. Be that as it may, UNIX itself was unquestionably increasingly costly. In journey of enormous cash, the UNIX sellers evaluated it sufficiently high to guarantee little pc clients avoided it. The source code of UNIX, once educated in universities kindness of Bell Labs, was presently circumspectly and not distributed openly. To add to the disappointment of pc clients around the world, the large players in the product showcase neglected to give an effective answer for this issue.

An answer appeared to show up in type of MINIX. It was composed without any preparation by Andrew S. Tanenbaum, a Dutch educaToR who needed to show his understudies the internal functions of a genuine operating system. It was intended to run on Intel 8086 microchips that had overflowed the world market.

As an operating system, MINIX was not a brilliant one. Yet, it had the bit of leeway that the source code was accessible. Any individual who happened to get the book 'operating System' by Tanenbaum could get hold of the 12,000 lines of code, written in c and low level computing construct. Just because, a hopeful developer or programmer could peruse the source codes of the operating system, which to that time the product merchants had watched overwhelmingly. Understudies of computer Science everywhere throughout the world poured over the book, perusing the codes to comprehend the very system that runs their pc. What's more is that one of them was Linus ToRvalds.

In 1991, Linus Benedict ToRvalds was a second year understudy of computer Science at the University of Helsinki and a self-trained programmer. The multi year old sandy haired mild-mannered Finn wanted to tinker with the intensity of the pcs and the points of confinement to which the system can be pushed. In any case, every one of that was missing was an operating system that could fulfil the needs of the experts. MINIX was great, yet it was basically an operating system for the understudies, planned as a display instrument as opposed to an industry quality one.

Around then, developers overall were incredibly roused by the GNU venture by Richard Stallman, a product development to give free and quality programming. The much anticipated Gnu c compiler was accessible by at that point, yet there was still no operating system. Indeed, even MINIX must be authorized. Work was going on the GNU bit HURD; however that shouldn't turn out inside a couple of years.

Linus himself didn't accept that his creation would have been large enough to change figuring until the end of time. Linux rendition 0.01 was released by mid September 1991, and was put on the net. excitement accumulated around this tenderfoot, and codes were downloaded, tried, changed, and came back to Linus. 0.02.

Also, Linux adaptation 0.03 arrived in half a month. By December came form 0.10. Still, Linux was minimal more than in skeletal structure. It had support for AT hard circles, had no login (booted straightforwardly to slam). Adaptation 0.11 was vastly improved with help for multilingual consoles, floppy circle drivers, and support for VGA, eGA, and Hercules and so on. The rendition numbers went legitimately from 0.12 to 0.95 and 0.96, etc. Before long the code went overall by means of ftp locales at Finland and somewhere else and in excess of a hundred people joined the Linux camp, at that point thousands, and afterward several thousands. This was never again a programmer's toy. controlled by a plenty of projects from the GNU venture, Linux was prepared for the genuine confrontation. It was authorized under GNU General public License, consequently guaranteeing that the source codes will be free for all to duplicate, study and to change. Understudies and software engineers got it.

Before long, business sellers moved in. Linux itself was, and is free. What the merchants did was to arrange up different programming and accumulate them in a distributed organization, increasingly like the other operating systems with which individuals were progressively well-known. Red Hat , caldera, Debian, and some different organizations increased generous measure of reaction from the clients around the world. With the new Graphical User Interfaces (like X-windows, KDe) the Linux circulations turned out to be mainstream.

The best thing about Linux today is the aficionado tailing it directions. At whatever point another bit of equipment is out, Linux part is changed to exploit it. For instance, inside weeks after the presentation of Intel Xeon® Microprocessor, Linux portion was changed and was prepared for it. It has additionally been adjusted for use in Alpha, Mac, powerpc, and in any event, for palmtops, an accomplishment which is not really coordinated by some other operating system. What's more, it proceeds with its voyage into the new millennium, with a similar eagerness that began one fine day in 1991.

From that point forward, Linux is serving to be one of the most well known operating systems, serving a few advantages as pursues:

- Being open-source, anybody with programming information can alter it.
    - The Linux operating systems presently offer a large number of projects/applications to browse the greater part of them free!
    - once you have Linux introduced you never again need an antivirus! Linux is an exceptionally secure system. All the more in this way, there is a worldwide advancement network continually seeing approaches to improve its security. With each redesign, the oS turns out to be increasingly secure and strong
    - Linux is the oS of decision for Server situations because of its solidness and unwavering quality (Mega-organizations like Amazon, Facebook, and Google use Linux for their Servers). A Linux based server could run constant without a reboot for quite a long time.

Figure 2. Linus Torvalds; the principal developer of Linux kernel.

chapter Two- Linux everyday

Something that separates Linux from other operating systems is how programming is introduced and oversaw. customarily when you needed to introduce programming on the Windows operating system you would discover the product, download the product, and introduce the product. These are steps that the end client needs to perform individually, imaging perusing the web for an application, downloading that application to your "Downloads" envelope, double tapping on the download to begin the establishment procedure and afterward responding to a progression of inquiries to at long last introduce the product.

To introduce programming on a Linux system you utilize the bundle administraToR that accompanies the circulation. To introduce another bit of programming you look for it and introduce it from the operating system itself. The bundle direcToR deals with downloading the ideal programming alongside any necessary conditions and afterward introduces the entirety of the parts. Not exclusively can bundle chiefs control applications, they can likewise deal with the operating system itself. A bundle chief can refresh and update the system and the entirety of its introduced applications to most recent adaptations.

programming and applications are packaged into bundles and Linux circulations are classified by these bundle types. The three essential sorts of bundles are Debian (deb), RedHat package Manager (RpM), and different appropriations.

Debian Based Linux Distributions

The deb bundle type was made in 1993 for the Debian Linux appropriation. Debian is one of most established Linux dispersions and it's a well known decision on which new circulations are based. Well known circulations that utilization .deb bundles include:
- Debian
- Ubuntu
- Linux Mint
- SteamoS

Debian

In 1993 Ian Murdock reported another Linux conveyance that should have been grown transparently with the GNU reasoning. Ian gave his dissemination the name Debian which is a mix of his sweetheart's name Debra and his own name. From the start it was a little undertaking, however today Debian is one of greatest open source extends in presence.

Debian is an all-inclusive operating system and supports practically all cpU structures and it is a well-known in the server space. In spite of the fact that Debian is known for unshakable stable programming, there are variations. There is Debian old steady, stable, testing, shaky and exploratory. As you go from old stable to exploratory, you find more current and less steady programming. With respect to bundle the executives, Debian utilizes two bundle directors, able and inclination.

Ubuntu

Reported in 2004, Ubuntu depends on Debian shaky. Ubuntu is the most generally utilized and most famous Linux circulation today. It's additionally the Linux dissemination encompassed by the most debates. Ubuntu began with the Gnome work area, however a couple of years back Ubuntu built up its very own work area condition named Unity. The Ubuntu establishment process is simple and along these lines is well known with those new to Linux. Ubuntu utilizes able and its graphical fronted Ubuntu Software center for bundle the executives.

Linux Mint

Linux Mint is a well-known dissemination dependent on Ubuntu. Mint began just being Ubuntu with pre-introduced interactive media codecs and exclusive drivers. Be that as it may, it has since developed and is an exceptionally famous option to Ubuntu.

RpM Based Linux Distributions

RedHat made the rpm bundle design for use in its circulation. Mainstream RpM based appropriations include:
- RedHat enterprise Linux (RHeL)
- centoS
- Fedora
- openSuse
- Mageia

Fedora

Fedora is the upstream of the business RedHat enterprise Linux circulation, or RHeL for short. What makes Fedora uncommon is it utilizes more up to date innovation and bundles from the open source world than RHeL. Fedora, as RHeL, utilizes the yum bundle administraToR.

openSuse

openSuse began a German interpretation of Slackware Linux, yet in the long run developed into its very own appropriation. openSuse is known for the KDe work area and dependability. For bundle the executives openSuse utilizes zypper and its graphical fronted, the Yast programming focus.

Mageia

Mageia Linux is a genuinely new Linux appropriation that depends on Mandrake Linux. Mageia is anything but difficult to introduce and simple to utilize. Mageia uses urpmi and drakrpm for bundle the board.

other Linux appropriations

curve Linux

curve Linux utilizes pkg.tar.xz bundles and has it's very own bundle supervisor called pacman. curve doesn't accompany a graphical installer and the entire establishment process is done by means of a terminal. This can be scary for new Linux clients. The principle theory behind Arch is KISS – keep it straightforward, moronic. curve has been forked in some well known novice cordial conveyances, for example, Manjaro Linux.

Slackware Linux

established in 1992 by patrick Volkerding, Slackware is the most established Linux appropriation being used today. Slackware doesn't have a bundle direcToR and all the product is accumulated by the system overseer or ordinary clients of the system. Slackware bundles are essentially source code. on the off chance that you truly need to become familiar with a great deal about the Linux truly works, use Slackware.

Gentoo Linux

Gentoo depends on the portage bundle the board system. Gentoo can be hard to introduce and can even take up to several days to finish the whole establishment process. The benefit of such a methodology is, that the product is worked for the particular equipment that it will be running on. Like Slackware, portage utilizes application source code. on the off chance that you like the possibility of Gentoo, yet are searching for something amateur inviting, attempt Sabayon.

Graphical User environments

While picking the correct Linux dispersion for you, it very well may be confounding given the assortment of decisions in work area direcToRs. While Microsoft Windows clients just have one work area supervisor, Linux clients can picked their work area condition. The work area condition, or the graphical UI (GUI), is what is shown on the screen. Said another way, it's the manner by which the system looks. Well known work area supervisors incorporate KDe, Gnome, Xfce, cinnamon and LXDe.

KDe

KDe was made in 1996 and is likely the most exceptional work area administraToR available. As a matter of course KDe incorporates a few applications that each client requirements for a total work area condition. KDe has a few highlights that are not accessible in other work area administraToRs. The KDe workspace is called plasma. Join plasma with the other KDe applications and you get what is known as the KDe programming accumulation, or KDe Sc for short.

Well known circulations that utilization KDe include:

- openSuse
- Slackware
- Linux Mint
- Kubuntu
- Mageia

Dwarf

Gnome is a work area administraToR made for the network and by the network. This is an extraordinary case of how the open source network functions. Gnome can undoubtedly be extended with the utilization of modules. It doesn't require a ton of assets and can be an extraordinary decision for more established and more slow equipment. Famous appropriations that utilization Gnome include:
- Debian
- openSuse
- Fedora
- centoS

cinnamon

cinnamon is a fork of the Gnome work area chief and is created by the Linux Mint people group. It reproduces the appearance of Gnome 2 with a cutting edge contact. The base system necessities for cinnamon are equivalent to they are for Gnome.

Xfce

Xfce is a superb decision for more established pcs. Light and quick are Xfce's two greatest highlights. The system necessities are a measly 300Mhz cpU and 192Mb of RAM. Well known appropriations that utilization Xfce include:
- Debian
- Xubuntu
- Fedora
- openSuse

LXDe

LXDe is an another quick and light work area chief. In light of the openBox windows direcToR, LXDe is reasonable for old pcs. Well known conveyances utilizing LXDe include:
- Lubuntu
- Debian
- openSuse
- Linux Mint

Unity

Unity was created by canonical for their Ubuntu Linux dispersion. Until now, Ubuntu is the main dispersion that utilizations Unity. Unity requires more noteworthy equipment assets than most graphical situations. You'll require a 1 GHz cpU and 1Gb RAM so as to get Unity to work. With those specs, Unity will be delayed to such an extent that it's practically unusable. For Unity, the more RAM and cpU, the better.

chapter Three - Installing Linux

In any operating system we have utilized in our pc, application or programming is the principle. In Windows, we download an .exe document and introduce it by clicking Next and introduce. Be that as it may, how to introduce programming in Linux?
Indeed, Linux has a few technique to introduce applications/programming. The content covered will show you around thirteen most straightforward steps to introducing programming on Linux. This is an extreme guide for tenderfoot to master clients.

1. **Downloading preferred Linux Distribution**

Download your preferred Linux distribution. In case you're new to Linux, think about attempting a lightweight and simple to utilize distribution, for example, Ubuntu or Linux Mint. Linux distributions (known as "distros") are ordinarily accessible for nothing to download in ISo position. You can discover your preferred ISo for the circulation at the distribution's site. This arrangement should be copied to a cD or USB stick before you can utilize it to introduce Linux. This will make a Live cD or Live USB.
A Live cD or Live USB is a circle that you can boot into, and regularly contains a see form of the operating system that can be run legitimately from the cD or USB stick.
Introduce a picture consuming project, or utilize your system's worked in consuming apparatus on the off chance that you are utilizing Windows 7, 8, or Mac oS X. pen Drive Linux and UNetBootin are two famous devices for consuming ISo records to USB sticks.

2. **Live cD/Live USB boot**

Boot into the Live cD or Live USB. Most pcs are set to boot into the hard drive first, which implies you should change a few settings to boot from your recently copied cD or USB. Start by rebooting the pc.
When the pc reboots, press the key used to enter the boot menu. The key for your system will be shown on a similar screen as the producer's logo. Run of the mill keys incorporate F12, F2, or Del.
For Windows 8 clients, hold the Shift key and snap restart. This will stack the Advanced Startup options, where you can boot from cD. For Windows 10 clients, go to cutting edge boot in settings and snap "Restart Now."
on the off chance that your pc doesn't give you direct access to the boot menu from the producer's sprinkle screen, it's probably covered up in the BIoS menu. You can get to the BIoS menu similarly that you would get to the boot menu. At the maker sprinkle screen, the key ought to be recorded in one of the base corners.
When you're in the boot menu, select your live cD or USB. When you've changed the settings, spare and leave the BIoS arrangement or boot menu. Your pc will proceed with the boot procedure.

3. **Linux Distribution Live environment**

evaluate the Linux distribution before introducing. Most Live cDs and USBs can dispatch a "live domain", enabling you to test it out before doing the switch. You won't have the option to make records, however you can explore around the interface and choose if it's appropriate for you.

4. The Installation process

Start the installation procedure. In case you're giving a shot the distro, you can dispatch the establishment from the application on the work area. on the off chance that you chose not to evaluate the appropriation, you can begin the establishment from the boot menu.

You will be approached to design some fundamental alternatives, for example, language, console format, and time zone.

5. enter your credentials

Make a username and secret key. You should make login data to introduce Linux. A secret word will be required to sign into your record and perform regulaToRy undertakings.

6. Segmentation

Linux should be introduced on a different segment from some other operating systems on your pc in the event that you plan double booting Linux with another oS. A segment is a part of the hard drive that is arranged explicitly for that operating system. You can skirt this progression on the off chance that you don't anticipate double booting.

Distros, for example, Ubuntu will set a suggested parcel naturally. You would then be able to alter this physically yourself. Most Linux establishments require at any rate 20 GB, so make certain to save enough space for both the Linux operating system and some other projects you may introduce and records you may make.

In the event that the establishment procedure doesn't give you programmed parcels, ensure that the segment you make is designed as ext4. on the off chance that the duplicate of Linux you are introducing is the main operating system on the pc, you will in all probability need to physically set your segment size.

7. Boot into Linux

When the establishment is done, your pc will reboot. You will see another screen when your pc boots up called "GNU GRUB". This is a boot loader that handles Linux establishments. pick your new Linux distro from the rundown. This screen may not appear on the off chance that you just make them work system on your pc. In the event that this screen isn't being introduced to you consequently, at that point you can get it back by hitting shift directly after the maker sprinkle screen.

on the off chance that you introduce numerous distros on your pc, they will all be recorded here.

8. checking your hardware

Most equipment should work out of the case with your Linux distro, however you may need to download some extra drivers to get everything working.

Some equipment requires exclusive drivers to work accurately in Linux. This is generally regular with illustrations cards. There is commonly an open source driver that will work, yet to take advantage of your designs cards you should download the exclusive drivers from the maker.

In Ubuntu, you can download exclusive drivers through the System Settings menu. Select the Additional Drivers alternative, and afterward select the illustrations driver from the rundown. Different distros have explicit strategies for getting additional drivers.
You can discover different drivers from this rundown too, for example, Wi-Fi drivers.

9. **Using Linux**

Start utilizing Linux. When your establishment is finished and you've checked that your equipment is working, you're prepared to begin utilizing Linux. Most distros accompany a few well known projects introduced, and you can download a lot more from their separate record vaults.

chapter Four-An Introduction to Kali Linux

Kali Linux is a Debian-based Linux conveyance went for cutting edge penetration Testing and Security Auditing. Kali contains a few hundred apparatuses which are outfitted towards different data security undertakings, for example, penetration Testing, Security investigate, computer Forensics and Reverse engineering. Kali Linux is created, supported and kept up by offensive Security, a main data security preparing organization.

Kali Linux was discharged on the thirteenth March, 2013 as a total, start to finish remake of BackTrack Linux, holding fast totally to Debian advancement norms.

More than 600 penetration testing tools included: After reviewing every tool that was included in BackTrack, we eliminated a great number of tools that either simply did not work or which duplicated other tools that provided the same or similar functionality. Details on what's included are on the Kali Tools site.

Free (as in beer) and always will be: Kali Linux, like BackTrack, is completely free of charge and always will be. You will never, ever have to pay for Kali Linux.

open source Git tree: We are committed to the open source development model and our development tree is available for all to see. All of the source code which goes into Kali Linux is available for anyone who wants to tweak or rebuild packages to suit their specific needs.

FHS compliant: Kali adheres to the Filesystem Hierarchy Standard, allowing Linux users to easily locate binaries, support files, libraries, etc.

Wide-ranging wireless device support: A regular sticking point with Linux distributions has been supported for wireless interfaces. We have built Kali Linux to support as many wireless devices as we possibly can, allowing it to run properly on a wide variety of hardware and making it compatible with numerous USB and other wireless devices.

custom kernel, patched for injection: As penetration testers, the development team often needs to do wireless assessments, so our kernel has the latest injection patches included.

Developed in a secure environment: The Kali Linux team is made up of a small group of individuals who are the only ones trusted to commit packages and interact with the repositories, all of which is done using multiple secure protocols.

GpG signed packages and repositories: every package in Kali Linux is signed by each individual developer who built and committed it, and the reposiToRies subsequently sign the packages as well.

Multi-language support: Although penetration tools tend to be written in english, we have ensured that Kali includes true multilingual support, allowing more users to operate in their native language and locate the tools they need for the job.

completely customizable: We thoroughly understand that not everyone will agree with our design decisions, so we have made it as easy as possible for our more adventurous users to customize Kali Linux to their liking, all the way down to the kernel.

ARMeL and ARMHF support: Since ARM-based single-board systems like the Raspberry pi and Beagl eBone Black, among others, are becoming more and more prevalent and inexpensive, we knew that Kali's ARM support would need to be as robust as we could manage, with fully working installations for both ARMeL and ARMHF systems. Kali Linux is available on a wide range of ARM devices and has ARM repositories integrated with the mainline distribution so tools for ARM are updated in conjunction with the rest of the distribution.

Kali Linux has not just become the data security expert's foundation of decision, yet advanced into a mechanical evaluation, and world-class working system dispersion - develop, secure, and endeavour prepared. As the decade progressed long advancement procedure, Muts and his group, alongside endless volunteers from the programmer network, have assumed the weight of streamlining and arranging our workplace, liberating us from a great part of the drudgery. They gave a protected and solid establishment, enabling us to focus on verifying our computerized world. An astounding network has developed around Kali Linux. consistently, more than 300,000 of us download an adaptation of Kali. We meet up in on the web and genuine preparing rooms and crush through the rambling offensive Security penetration Testing Labs, seeking after the close unbelievable offensive Security confirmations. We meet up on the Kali gatherings, nearly 40,000 in number, and many us one after another can be found on the Kali IRc channel. We assemble at gatherings and go to Kali Dojos to gain from the engineers themselves how to best use Kali. Be that as it may, the Kali group has never discharged an official Kali Linux manual, as of recently. In this book, we'll centre around the Kali Linux stage itself, and assist you with comprehension and augment Kali starting from the earliest stage. The designers will walk you through Kali Linux highlights and essentials, give an intense training in fundamental Linux directions and ideas, and afterward walk you through the most well-known Kali Linux establishment situations. You'll figure out how to design, investigate and verify Kali Linux and afterward plunge into the incredible Debian bundle chief. All through this broad area, you'll figure out how to introduce and design bundles, how to refresh and update your Kali establishment, and how to make your very own custom bundles. At that point you'll figure out how to convey your custom establishment crosswise over gigantic undertaking systems. At last, you'll be guided through cutting edge themes, for example, piece assemblage, custom ISo creation, mechanical quality encryption, and even how to introduce crypto off buttons to shield your touchy data. Regardless of whether you're a veteran or a flat out n00b, this is the best spot to begin with Kali Linux, the security expert's foundation of decision.

So as to run Kali "Live" from a USB drive on standard Windows and Apple pcs, you'll need a Kali Linux bootable ISo picture, in either 32-piece or 64-piece position.

In case you don't know of the design of the system you need to run Kali on, on Linux or mac oS, you can run the order uname - m at the direction line. on the off chance that you get the reaction, "x86_64", utilize the 64-piece ISo picture (the one containing "amd64" in the record name); in the event that you get "i386", utilize the 32-piece picture (the one containing "i386" in the document name). In case you're on a Windows system, the technique for deciding if your engineering is nitty gritty on Microsoft's site.

VMware Images

on the off chance that you need to run Kali Linux as a "visitor" under VMware, Kali is accessible as a pre-manufactured VMware virtual machine with VMware Tools previously introduced. The VMware picture is accessible in a 64-piece (amd64), 32-piece (i686), and 32-piece pAe (i486) positions.

ARM Images

The equipment designs of ARM-based gadgets differ impressively, so it is preposterous to expect to have a solitary picture that will work over every one of them. pre-manufactured Kali Linux pictures for the ARM design are accessible for a wide scope of gadgets.

contents for building your very own ARM pictures locally are additionally accessible on GitLab. For more subtleties, see the articles on setting up an ARM cross-gathering condition and building a custom Kali Linux ARM chroot.

Before you run Kali Linux Live, or introduce it to your hard plate, you need to be exceptionally certain that what you have really is Kali Linux, and not a fraud. Kali Linux is an expert entrance testing and criminology toolbox. As an expert entrance analyzer, having outright trust in the honesty of your devices is basic: if your instruments aren't dependable, your examinations won't be reliable, either.

Additionally, as the main infiltration testing appropriation, Kali's qualities imply that a fake rendition of Kali Linux could do a colossal measure of harm on the off chance that it were conveyed accidentally. There are a lot of individuals with a lot of motivation to need to stick crude stuff into something that resembles Kali, and you totally would prefer not to wind up running something to that effect.

Just download Kali Linux by means of the authority download pages at https://www.kali.org/downloads or https://www.offensive-security.com/kali-linux-vmware-arm-picture download/ — you won't have the option to peruse to these pages without SSL; scrambling the association makes it a lot harder for an assailant to utilize a "man-in-the-centre" assault to alter your download. There are a couple of potential shortcomings to even these sources — see the areas on checking the download with the SHA256SUMS document and its mark against the official Kali Development group private key for something a lot nearer to outright confirmation.
When you've downloaded a picture, and before you run it, generally approve that it truly is what it should be by confirming its checksum utilizing one of the strategies point by point beneath.
There are a few techniques for confirming your download. each gives a specific degree of affirmation, and includes a comparing level of exertion on your part.

You can download an ISo picture from an official Kali Linux "Downloads" reflect, compute the ISo's SHA256 hash and contrast it by assessment and the worth recorded on the Kali Linux website. This is speedy and simple, however possibly defenceless to disruption by means of a DNS harming: it accept that the site to which, for instance, the space "kali.org" settle is in certainty the genuine Kali Linux site. In the event that it by one way or another weren't, an aggressor could show a "stacked" picture and a coordinating SHA256 signature on the phony website page. See the area "physically Verify the Signature on the ISo (Direct Download)", underneath.

You can download an ISo picture through the deluges, and it will likewise pull down a record — unsigned — containing the determined SHA256 signature. You would then be able to utilize the shasum direction (on Linux and macOS) or an utility (on Windows) to naturally confirm that the record's registered mark coordinates the mark in the optional document. This is significantly simpler than the "manual" technique, yet experiences a similar shortcoming: if the downpour you pulled down isn't generally Kali Linux, it could in any case have a decent signature. See the segment "check the Signature on the ISo Using the Included Signature File (Torrent Download)", underneath.

To be as near sure beyond a shadow of a doubt as conceivable that the Kali Linux download you've gotten is the genuine article, you can download both a clear text signature record and variant of a similar document that has been marked with the official Kali Linux private key and use GNU privacy Guard (GpG) to first, confirm that the figured SHA256 signature and the mark in the clear text record match and second, check that the marked rendition of the record containing the SHA256 hash has been effectively marked with the official key.

In the event that you utilize this increasingly confounded process and effectively approve your downloaded ISo, you can continue with entirely complete confirmation that what you have is the official picture and that it has not been altered at all. This technique, while the most intricate, has the upside of giving autonomous affirmation of the respectability of the picture. The main way this strategy can come up short is if the official Kali Linux private key isn't just subverted by an aggressor, yet in addition not along these lines renounced by the Kali Linux improvement group. For this technique, see the segment on check utilizing the SHA256SUMS record.

In case you're running on Linux, you most likely as of now have GpG (GNU privacy Guard) introduced. In case you're on Windows or mac oS, you'll have to introduce the fitting variant for your foundation.

In case you're on a pc running Windows, download and introduce GpG4Win from here. Since Windows doesn't have the local capacity to figure SHA256 checksums, you will likewise require an utility, for example, Microsoft File checksum Integrity Verifier or Hashtab to confirm your download.

In case you're on a Macintosh running macOS, download and introduce GpG Tools from here. on the other hand, on the off chance that you have Homebrew introduced, simply run mix introduce gnupg

When you've introduced GpG, you'll have to download and import a duplicate of the Kali Linux official key. Do this with the accompanying direction:

```
$ wget -q -o - https://archive.kali.org/archive-key.asc | gpg --import
```

or

```
$ gpg --keyserver hkp://keys.gnupg.net --recv-key 44c6513A8e4FB3D30875F758eD444FF07D8D0BF6
```

Your output should look like this:

```
gpg: key eD444FF07D8D0BF6: public key "Kali Linux ReposiToRy <devel@kali.org>" imported
gpg: Total number processed: 1
gpg: imported: 1 (RSA: 1)
```

Verify that the key is properly installed with the command:

```
$ gpg --fingerprint 44c6513A8e4FB3D30875F758eD444FF07D8D0BF6
```

The output will look like this:

```
pub rsa4096 2012-03-05 [Sc] [expires: 2021-02-03]
      44c6 513A 8e4F B3D3 0875 F758 eD44 4FF0 7D8D 0BF6
uid [ full ] Kali Linux ReposiToRy <devel@kali.org>
sub rsa4096 2012-03-05 [e] [expires: 2021-02-03]
```

You're now set up to validate your Kali Linux download.

chapter Five- Making Kali a USB Bootable Device

our preferred way, and the quickest strategy, for getting going with Kali Linux is to run it "live" from a USB drive. This strategy has a few points of interest:
It's non-ruinous — it rolls out no improvements to the host system's hard drive or introduced oS, and to return to ordinary activities, you just expel the "Kali Live" USB drive and restart the system.
It's versatile — you can convey Kali Linux in your pocket and make them run in minutes on an accessible system
It's adjustable — you can roll your own custom Kali Linux ISo picture and put it onto a USB drive utilizing similar techniques
It's conceivably industrious — with a touch of additional exertion, you can design your Kali Linux "live" USB drive to have tireless stockpiling, so the information you gather is spared crosswise over reboots
So as to do this, we first need to make a bootable USB drive which has been set up from an ISo picture of Kali Linux.

Requirements to perform the task

A checked duplicate of the suitable ISo picture of the most recent Kali manufacture picture for the system you'll be running it on: see the subtleties on downloading official Kali Linux pictures.
In case you're running under Windows, you'll additionally need to download the etcher imaging device. on Linux and oS X, you can utilize the dd order, which is pre-introduced on those stages, or use etcher.
A USB thumb drive, 4GB or bigger. (Systems with an immediate SD card space can utilize a SD card with comparative limit. The strategy is indistinguishable.)

creating a bootable Kali device on Windows

1. plug your USB crash into an accessible USB port on your Windows pc, note which drive designate (for example "F:\") it utilizes once it mounts, and dispatch etcher.
2. pick the Kali Linux ISo document to be imaged with "select picture" and check that the USB drive to be overwritten is the right one. Snap the "Streak!" button once prepared.
3. When etcher alarms you that the picture has been flashed, you can securely evacuate the USB drive and continue to boot into Kali with it.

creating a bootable Kali device on Linux

Making a bootable Kali Linux USB key in a Linux domain is simple. When you've downloaded and checked your Kali ISo document, you can utilize the dd direction to duplicate it over to your USB stick utilizing the accompanying system. Note that you'll should be running as root, or to execute the dd direction with sudo. The accompanying model accept a Linux Mint 17.1 work area — relying upon the distro you're utilizing, a couple of points of interest may shift marginally, yet the general thought ought to be fundamentally the same as. In the event that you would like to utilize etcher, at that point pursue indistinguishable headings from a Windows client. Note that the USB drive will have a way like/dev/sdb.

1. To start with, you'll have to recognize the gadget way to use to compose the picture to your USB drive. Without the USB drive embedded into a port, execute the direction sudo fdisk - l at an order brief in a terminal window (on the off chance that you don't utilize raised benefits with fdisk, you won't get any yield). You'll get yield that will look something (not actually) like this, demonstrating a solitary drive — "/dev/sda" — containing three parcels (/dev/sda1,/dev/sda2, and/dev/sda5):

```
mcfate@McFateMint ~ $ sudo fdisk -l

Disk /dev/sda: 68.7 GB, 68719476736 bytes
255 heads, 63 sectors/track, 8354 cylinders, total 134217728 sectors
Units = sectors of 1 * 512 = 512 bytes
Sector size (logical/physical): 512 bytes / 4096 bytes
I/O size (minimum/optimal): 4096 bytes / 4096 bytes
Disk identifier: 0x000650d7

   Device Boot      Start         End      Blocks   Id  System
/dev/sda1   *        2048   132120575    66059264   83  Linux
/dev/sda2          132122622  134215679    1046529    5  Extended
Partition 2 does not start on physical sector boundary.
/dev/sda5          132122624  134215679    1046528   82  Linux swap / Solaris
mcfate@McFateMint ~ $
```

2. presently, plug your USB crash into an accessible USB port on your framework, and run a similar order, "sudo fdisk - l" a subsequent time. presently, the yield will look something (once more, not actually) like this, demonstrating an extra gadget which wasn't there beforehand, in this model "/dev/sdb", a 16GB USB drive:

```
Disk /dev/sda: 68.7 GB, 68719476736 bytes
255 heads, 63 sectors/track, 8354 cylinders, total 134217728 sectors
Units = sectors of 1 * 512 = 512 bytes
Sector size (logical/physical): 512 bytes / 4096 bytes
I/O size (minimum/optimal): 4096 bytes / 4096 bytes
Disk identifier: 0x000650d7

   Device Boot      Start         End      Blocks   Id  System
/dev/sda1   *        2048    132120575    66059264   83  Linux
/dev/sda2        132122622    134215679     1046529    5  Extended
Partition 2 does not start on physical sector boundary.
/dev/sda5        132122624    134215679     1046528   82  Linux swap / Solaris

Disk /dev/sdb: 15.6 GB, 15610576896 bytes
179 heads, 32 sectors/track, 5322 cylinders, total 30489408 sectors
Units = sectors of 1 * 512 = 512 bytes
Sector size (logical/physical): 512 bytes / 512 bytes
I/O size (minimum/optimal): 512 bytes / 512 bytes
Disk identifier: 0x73876c0c

   Device Boot      Start         End      Blocks   Id  System
/dev/sdb1   *          64     5836831     2918384   17  Hidden HPFS/NTFS
/dev/sdb2          5836832     5963615       63392    1  FAT12
mcfate@McFateMint ~ $ ls -l
```

3. continue to (deliberately!) picture the Kali ISo document on the USB gadget. The model order underneath expect that the ISo picture you're composing is named "kali-linux-2019.4-amd64.iso" and is in your present working catalog. The blocksize parameter can be expanded, and keeping in mind that it might accelerate the activity of the dd order, it can every so often produce unbootable USB drives, contingent upon your framework and a variety of components. The suggested worth, "bs=512k", is traditionalist and dependable.
   dd if=kali-linux-2019.4-amd64.iso of=/dev/sdb bs=512k

dd if=kali-linux-2019.4-amd64.iso of=/dev/sdb bs=512k

Imaging the USB drive can take a decent measure of time, more than ten minutes or more isn't unordinary, as the example yield beneath appears. Show restraint!
The direction gives no criticism until it's finished, however on the off chance that your drive has an entrance marker, you'll likely observe it glinting every now and then. The opportunity to dd the picture crosswise over will rely upon the speed of the framework utilized, USB drive itself, and USB port it's embedded into. When dd has wrapped up the drive, it will yield something that resembles this:
5823+1 records in
5823+1 records out
3053371392 bytes (3.1 GB) copied, 746.211 s, 4.1 MB/s

Your device is now ready to be booted.
creating a bootable Kali USB Drive on oS X

operating system X depends on UNIX, so making a bootable Kali Linux USB drive in an oS X condition is like doing it on Linux. When you've downloaded and checked your picked Kali ISo document, you use dd to duplicate it over to your USB stick. on the off chance that you would like to utilize etcher, at that point pursue indistinguishable bearings from a Windows client. Note that the USB drive will have a way like/dev/disk2.

1. Without the USB drive connected to the framework, open a Terminal window, and type the direction diskutil list at the order brief.
2. You will get a rundown of the gadget ways (looking like/dev/rdisk0,/dev/rdisk1, and so forth.) of the circles mounted on your framework, alongside data on the allotments on every one of the plates.

```
/dev/disk1
   #:                       TYPE NAME                    SIZE       IDENTIFIER
   0:                   Apple_HFS Macintosh HD          *499.0 GB   disk1
                                  Logical Volume on disk0s2
                                  51531BD1-8924-4285-AB42-3AB73A6510A6
                                  Unlocked Encrypted
/dev/disk2
   #:                       TYPE NAME                    SIZE       IDENTIFIER
   0:      Apple_partition_scheme                       *1.0 TB     disk2
   1:         Apple_partition_map                        32.3 KB    disk2s1
   2:                   Apple_HFS Unobtanium             1.0 TB     disk2s3
/dev/disk3
   #:                       TYPE NAME                    SIZE       IDENTIFIER
   0:      FDisk_partition_scheme                       *3.0 TB     disk3
   1:                   Apple_HFS Vibranium              3.0 TB     disk3s1
/dev/disk4
   #:                       TYPE NAME                    SIZE       IDENTIFIER
   0:      FDisk_partition_scheme                       *2.0 TB     disk4
   1:                   Apple_HFS Adamantium             2.0 TB     disk4s1
/dev/disk5
   #:                       TYPE NAME                    SIZE       IDENTIFIER
   0:       GUID_partition_scheme                       *290.1 MB   disk5
   1:                   Apple_HFS Parallels Access       290.1 MB   disk5s1
Huginn:~ mcfate$
```

1. Attachment in your USB gadget to your Apple pc's USB port and run the order diskutil list a subsequent time. Your USB drive's way will no doubt be the last one. Regardless, it will be one which was absent previously. In this model, you can see that there is currently a/dev/disk6 which wasn't already present.

```
                            51531BD1-8924-4285-AB42-3AB73A6510A6
                                    Unlocked Encrypted
/dev/disk2
   #:                      TYPE NAME                     SIZE           IDENTIFIER
   0:      Apple_partition_scheme                       *1.0 TB         disk2
   1:         Apple_partition_map                       32.3 KB         disk2s1
   2:                 Apple_HFS Unobtanium               1.0 TB         disk2s3
/dev/disk3
   #:                      TYPE NAME                     SIZE           IDENTIFIER
   0:      FDisk_partition_scheme                       *3.0 TB         disk3
   1:                 Apple_HFS Vibranium                3.0 TB         disk3s1
/dev/disk4
   #:                      TYPE NAME                     SIZE           IDENTIFIER
   0:      FDisk_partition_scheme                       *2.0 TB         disk4
   1:                 Apple_HFS Adamantium               2.0 TB         disk4s1
/dev/disk5
   #:                      TYPE NAME                     SIZE           IDENTIFIER
   0:       GUID_partition_scheme                       *290.1 MB       disk5
   1:                 Apple_HFS Parallels Access         290.1 MB       disk5s1
/dev/disk6
   #:                      TYPE NAME                     SIZE           IDENTIFIER
   0:      FDisk_partition_scheme                       *15.6 GB        disk6
   1:            Windows_FAT_32 KINGSTON                 15.6 GB        disk6s1
Huginn:~ mcfate$
```

1. Unmount the drive (expecting, for this model, the USB stick is/dev/disk6 — don't just duplicate this, confirm the right way without anyone else framework!):

`diskutil unmount /dev/disk6`

2. continue to (deliberately!) picture the Kali ISo document on the USB gadget. The accompanying order accept that your USB drive is on the way/dev/disk6, and you're in a similar index with your Kali Linux ISo, which is named "kali-linux-2019.4-amd64.iso":

`sudo dd if=kali-linux-2019.4-amd64.iso of=/dev/disk6 bs=1m`

Imaging the USB drive can take a decent measure of time, over 30 minutes isn't unordinary, as the example yield beneath appears. Show restraint!
The dd order gives no criticism until it's finished, yet in the event that your drive has an entrance pointer, you'll most likely observe it gleaming every once in a while. The opportunity to dd the picture crosswise over will rely upon the speed of the framework utilized, USB drive itself, and USB port it's embedded into. When dd has wrapped up the drive, it will yield something that resembles this:

```
2911+1 records in
2911+1 records out
3053371392 bytes transferred in 2151.132182 secs (1419425 bytes/sec)
```

What's more, that is it! You would now be able to boot into a Kali Live/Installer condition utilizing the USB gadget.
To boot from a substitute drive on an oS X framework, raise the boot menu by squeezing the option key following fuelling on the gadget and select the drive you need to utilize.

The following strategy shows a case of building a genuinely conventional Kali armhf rootfs. on the off chance that you wish to work for armel, utilize that worth instead of "armhf" when you send out the design condition variable.

Before we stroll through our model, it's presumably great to perceive how a custom ARM fabricate would really be practiced. ordinarily, to do a neighborhood work of a picture for, e.g., Raspberry pi, the procedure would be something like the accompanying. As an underlying one-time set-up, clone the ARM assemble contents vault on GitHub and introduce the fabricate essentials:

```
cd ~
git clone https://gitlab.com/kalilinux/build-scripts/kali-arm.git
dpkg --add-architecture i386
apt update
apt -y install debootstrap qemu-user-static device-tree-compiler lzma lzop u-boot-tools libncurses5:i386 pixz
```

To do an ARM construct, you should empower cross-aggregation for your present shell session:

```
export ARcH=arm
mkdir -p arm-stuff/kernel/toolchains
cd arm-stuff/kernel/toolchains
git clone git://gitlab.com/kalilinux/packages/gcc-arm-eabi-linaro-4-6-2.git
export cRoSS_coMpILe=~/arm-stuff/kernel/toolchains/gcc-arm-eabi-linaro-4.6.2/bin/arm-eabi-
```

At that point just conjure the construct content for the particular stage. Thus, for a Raspberry pi work of Kali Linux 2016.2, execute the directions:

```
cd ~
kali-arm-build-scripts/rpi.sh 2016.2
```

The ARM construct contents are for the most part totally independent, beside the underlying one-time establishment of the assemble essentials. The first occasion when you run one of the ARM assemble contents, it is critical that you assess the yield for any mistakes, for example, missing devices, and so forth., right them, and afterward re-run the content until you get a perfect form. Just by then would you be able to proceed to make any customizations you need to the fundamental form content to make the particular "formula" you're after.

It's conceivable to accelerate your works by storing the bundles you download utilizing adept cacher-ng, as portrayed in the past article. Note this can break a portion of the standard form contents except if you uncomment certain lines before building — they're noted in the contents themselves. In case you're utilizing adept cacher-ng, ensure you check your contents for any vital changes.

For solid and unsurprising outcomes, assemble your Kali Linix ARM chroot from inside a prior and state-of-the-art Kali Linux condition. This guide expect that you have just set up your ARM cross-arrangement condition.

To continue further, let us visualize an example of a Generic ARM Build of Kali Linux:
The manufacture portrayed here is both negligible and nonexclusive. Few essential bundles are incorporated, and the fuller setup required for a true stage is precluded for clearness. Utilize this model as a kind of perspective for understanding what's happening in the official ARM construct contents and as an elevated level guide for composing your own form contents. It tends to be effectively pursued as an independent instructional exercise from the order line, yet the picture delivered isn't probably going to run on a specific gadget. Utilize the pre-moved form contents, either as-is or with your very own customizations, to deliver working pictures for solid equipment.

1. Install dependencies first:

```
apt install de-bootstrap qemu-user-static
```

So as to empower the Linaro cross-aggregation, you should set these condition variable toward the start of each session.

2. enabling cross- compilation

So as to empower the Linaro cross-accumulation, you should set these condition variable toward the start of each session.

```
export ARcH=arm
export cRoSS_coMpILe=~/arm-stuff/kernel/toolchains/gcc-arm-eabi-linaro-4.6.2/bin/arm-eabi-
```

3. Defining Architecture and custom packages

This is the place you characterize some condition factors for your necessary ARM design (armel versus armhf) and list the bundles to be introduced in your picture. These will be utilized all through this article, so make a point to alter them to your needs.

```
export packages="xfce4 kali-menu wpa supplicant kali-defaults initramfs-tools u-boot-tools nmap openssh-server"
export architecture="armhf"
```

4. Set Up the Base rootfs

As our beginning stage, we'll make a standard registry structure and use debootstrap to introduce a base ARM rootfs from the Kali Linux archives. We at that point duplicate over qemu-arm-static, an ARM emulator, from our host machine into the rootfs so as to start the second stage chroot.

```
cd ~
mkdir -p arm-stuff # should have already been created when setting up x-compilation
cd arm-stuff/
mkdir -p kernel # should have already been created when setting up x-compilation
mkdir -p rootfs
cd rootfs
debootstrap --foreign --arch $architecture kali-rolling kali-$architecture http://http.kali.org/kali
cp /usr/bin/qemu-arm-static kali-$architecture/usr/bin/
```

5. Second Stage chroot

To start with, we'll chroot into our recently made base rootfs, use de-bootstrap a subsequent time to build our second-arrange rootfs, and design base picture settings, for example, stores (in/and so on/well-suited/sources.list), have name (in/and so on/hostname), default organize interfaces and conduct (in/and so on/organize/interfaces and/and so on/resolv.conf), and so forth. change these to suit your necessities.

```
cd ~/arm-stuff/rootfs
LANG=c chroot kali-$architecture /debootstrap/debootstrap --second-stage
cat kali-$architecture/etc/apt/sources.list
deb http://http.kali.org/kali kali-rolling main non-free contrib
# deb-src http://http.kali.org/kali kali-rolling main non-free contrib
eoF
echo "kali" > kali-$architecture/etc/hostname
cat kali-$architecture/etc/network/interfaces
auto lo
iface lo inet loopback
auto eth0
iface eth0 inet dhcp
eoF
cat kali-$architecture/etc/resolv.conf
nameserver 8.8.8.8
eoF
```

6. Third Stage chroot

This is the place your particular customizations come in. Your $packages list is introduced, as are key maps, a default root secret phrase of "tour" is set, and other arrangement changes and fixes are applied.

```
export MALLoc0 # workaround for Lp: #520465
export Lc_ALL=c
export DeBIAN_FRoNTeND=noninteractive
mount -t proc proc kali-$architecture/proc
mount -o bind /dev/ kali-$architecture/dev/
mount -o bind /dev/pts kali-$architecture/dev/pts
cat kali-$architecture/debconf.set
console-common console-data/keymap/policy select Select keymap from full list
console-common console-data/keymap/full select en-latin1-nodeadkeys
eoF

cat << eoF > kali-$architecture/third-stage
#!/bin/bash
dpkg-divert --add --local --divert /usr/sbin/invoke-rc.d.chroot --rename /usr/sbin/invoke-rc.d
cp /bin/true /usr/sbin/invoke-rc.d
apt update
apt install locales-all
```

```
#locale-gen en_US.UTF-8
debconf-set-selections /debconf.set
rm -f /debconf.set
apt update
apt -y install git-core binutils ca-certificates initramfs-tools u-boot-tools
apt -y install locales console-common less nano git
echo "root:toor" | chpasswd
sed -i -e 's/KeRNeL\!=\"eth\*|/KeRNeL\!=\"/' /lib/udev/rules.d/75-persistent-net-generaToR.rules
rm -f /etc/udev/rules.d/70-persistent-net.rules
apt-get --yes --force-yes install $packages
rm -f /usr/sbin/invoke-rc.d
dpkg-divert --remove --rename /usr/sbin/invoke-rc.d
rm -f /third-stage
eoF
chmod +x kali-$architecture/third-stage
LANG=c chroot kali-$architecture /third-stage
```

7. on the off chance that you have to make any further alterations in your rootfs condition, you can do as such by physically chrooting into it with the accompanying direction and rolling out any required improvements.

```
LANG=c chroot kali-$architecture
```

When you've finished your alterations, leave the chroot'ed rootfs with the order:

```
exit
```

8. Finally, we make and run a clean up content in our chroot to free up space utilized by stored documents and run some other clean up occupations we may require, and unmount the indexes we were utilizing in our rootfs.

```
cat << eoF > kali-$architecture/cleanup
#!/bin/bash
rm -rf /root/.bash_hisToRy
apt update
apt clean
rm -f cleanup
eoF
chmod +x kali-$architecture/cleanup
LANG=c chroot kali-$architecture /cleanup
umount kali-$architecture/proc
umount kali-$architecture/dev/pts
umount kali-$architecture/dev/
cd ..
```

congrats! Your custom Kali ARM rootfs is situated in the ~/arm-stuff/rootfs/kali-$architecture catalogue. You would now be able to tar up this index or convert it to a picture document for further work.

chapter Six – The most popular Kali Linux tools

For simplicity of reference, we'll partition the most-utilized programming of Kali Linux into five particular classes: data gathering, helplessness examining, remote investigation instruments, secret phrase saltines, abuse devices and stress testing.

1. Nmap

Nmap is the world's most acclaimed system mapper apparatus. It enables you to find dynamic has inside any system, and procure other data, (for example, open ports) pertinent to entrance testing.

principle highlights:
- Host disclosure: valuable for recognizing has in any system
- port checking: lets you list open ports on the neighbourhood or remote host
- operating system identification: helpful for getting working framework and equipment data about any associated gadget
- Application rendition discovery: enables you to decide application name and form number
- Scriptable association: expands Nmap default abilities by utilizing Nmap Scripting engine (NSe)

[securitytrails@kali root]$ nmap --help Usage: nmap [Scan Type(s)] [options] {target specification} TARGeT SpecIFIcATIoN: can pass hostnames, Ip addresses, networks, etc. ex: scanme.nmap.org, microsoft.com/24, 192.168.0.1; 10.0.0-255.1-254 -iL <inputfilename>: Input from list of hosts/networks -iR <num hosts>: choose random targets --exclude <host1[,host2][,host3],...>: exclude hosts/networks --excludefile <exclude_file>: exclude list from file HoST DIScoVeRY: -sL: List Scan - simply list targets to scan -sn: ping Scan - disable port scan -pn: Treat all hosts as online -- skip host discovery -pS/pA/pU/pY[portlist]: Tcp SYN/AcK, UDp or ScTp discovery to given ports -pe/pp/pM: IcMp echo, timestamp, and netmask request discovery probes -po[protocol list]: Ip protocol ping -n/-R: Never do DNS resolution/Always resolve [default: sometimes] --dns-servers <serv1[,serv2],...>: Specify custom DNS servers --system-dns: Use oS's DNS resolver --traceroute: Trace hop path to each host

2. Netcat

Netcat is a system investigation application that isn't just well known among those in the security business, yet additionally in the system and framework organization fields.
While it's basically utilized for outbound/inbound system checking and port investigation, it's additionally important when utilized related to programming dialects like perl or c, or with slam contents.
Netcat's principle highlights include:
- Tcp and UDp port examination

- Inbound and outbound system sniffing
- Turn around and forward DNS investigation
- output neighbourhood and remote ports
- completely incorporated with terminal standard info
- UDp and Tcp burrowing mode

3. Unicornscan

Authorized under the GpL permit, Unicornscan is a standout amongst other infosec instruments utilized for data social occasion and information relationship. It offers progressed non-concurring Tcp and UDp examining highlights alongside extremely valuable system disclosure designs that will assist you with finding remote hosts. It can likewise uncover insights regarding the product running by every last one of them.

primary highlights include:
- Tcp no concurrent filter
- offbeat UDp examine
- offbeat Tcp pennant discovery
- operating system, application and framework administration location
- capacity to utilize custom informational collections
- Backing for SQL social yield

4. Fierce

Fierce is an incredible device for organize mapping and port checking. It very well may be utilized to find non-bordering Ip space and hostnames crosswise over systems.

It's like Nmap and Unicornscan, yet dissimilar to those, Fierce is for the most part utilized for explicit corporate systems.

When the entrance analyser has characterized the objective system, Fierce will run a few tests against the chose spaces to recover significant data that can be utilized for later investigation and abuse.

Its highlights include:
- capacity to change DNS server for switch queries
- Inner and outer Ip ranges filtering
- Ip range and whole class c checking
- Logs capacities into a framework document
- Name Servers disclosure and Zone Transfer assault
- Animal power abilities utilizing worked in or custom content rundown

5. openVAS

openVAS (open Vulnerability Assessment System) was created by part of the group liable for the well-known Nessus powerlessness scanner. Authorized under the GLp permit, it's free programming that anybody can use to investigate neighbourhood or remote system vulnerabilities.

This security instrument enables you to compose and coordinate your very own security modules to the openVAS stage — despite the fact that the present motor accompanies more than 50k NVTs (Network Vulnerability Tests) that can actually examine anything you envision as far as security vulnerabilities.

principle highlights:
- Synchronous host disclosure
- System mapper and port scanner
- Backing for openVAS Transfer protocol
- completely incorporated with SQL Databases like SQLite
- planned every day or week by week checks
- Fares results into XML, HTML, Latex document positions
- capacity to stop, respite and resume checks
- Full help for Linux and Windows
- openVAS Kali screen capture

6. Nikto

Written in perl and associated with Kali Linux, Nikto iworks as an enhancement to openVAS and different weakness scanners.

Nikto grants penetration analysers and good developers to play out a full web server clear to discover security blemishes and vulnerabilities. This security channel amasses results by distinguishing unstable record and application structures, old server programming and default archive names similarly as server and programming misconfigurations.

It joins support for delegates, have based approval, SSL encryption and significantly more.

Key features include:
- Breadths different ports on a server
- IDS evasion frameworks
- Yields results into TXT, XML, HTML, NBe or cSV.
- Apache and cgiwrap username list
- Recognizes presented programming by methods for headers, favicons and records
- Scopes showed cGI files
- Usages specially craft records
- Research and verbose yield.

7. WpScan

WpScan is endorsed for checking on your Wordpress foundation security. By using WpScan you can check if your Wordpress course of action is defenceless against explicit sorts of attacks, or if it's revealing an extreme measure of information in your inside, module or theme records.

This Wordpress security instrument in like manner lets you find any weak passwords for each and every enlisted customer, and even run a creature control attack against it to see which ones can be part.

WpScan gets visit invigorates from the wpvulndb.com Wordpress vulnerability database, which makes it an exceptional programming for present day Wp security.

What might you have the option to do with WpScan?
- Non-meddling security checks
- Wp username distinguishing proof
- Wp brute force attack and weak mystery key breaking

- Wp modules weakness detail
- Timetable Wordpress security checks

It is protected to state that you are enthused about Wordpress security? Take a gander at our blog section on asking definitely that: Is Wordpress secure?8. cMSMap

Not at all like WpScan, has cMSMap expected to be a concentrated answer for one, however up to four of the most mainstream cMS as far as defencelessness discovery.

cMSmap is an open source venture written in python that robotizes the procedure of weakness examining and recognition in Wordpress, Joomla, Drupal, and Moodle.

This device isn't valuable for distinguishing security defects in these four well known cMS yet additionally for running genuine animal power assaults and propelling adventures once a powerlessness has been found.

principle highlights include:
- Supports numerous sweep dangers
- capacity to set custom client operator and header
- Backing for SSL encryption.
- Verbose mode for investigating purposes
- Spares yield in a book record.

9. Fluxion

Fluxion is a Wi-Fi analyser that spends significant time in MITM WpA assaults.

It enables you to check remote systems, scanning for security blemishes in corporate or individual systems.

Not at all like other Wi-Fi breaking apparatuses, Fluxion doesn't dispatch any animal power splitting endeavours that normally take a great deal of time.

Rather, it generates a MDK3 procedure which powers all clients associated with the objective system to authenticate. When this is done, the client is provoked to interface with a phony passage, where they will enter the WiFi secret word. At that point the program reports the secret word to you, so you can obtain entrance.

10. Aircrack-ng

Aircrack-ng is a remote security programming suite. It involves a framework bundle analyzer, a Wep organize saltine, and WpA/WpA2-pSK nearby another course of action of remote looking at gadgets. Here are the most standard instruments associated with the Aircrack-ng suite:

Airmon-Ng: changes over your remote card into a remote card in an unpredictable way

Airmon-Ng: gets packs of needed detail, and t is particularly useful in disentangling passwords

Aircrack-Ng: used to unscramble passwords — prepared to use quantifiable methodology to unravel Wep and word references for WpA and WpA2 in the wake of getting the WpA handshake

Aireplay-Ng: can be used to make or stimulate traffic in a way

Airdecap-Ng: unscrambles remote traffic once we the key is deciphered

Fundamental highlights:
- Backing for Wep, WpA/WpA2-pSK passwords
- Quick Wep and WpA secret key decoding

- parcel sniffer and injector
- capacity to make a virtual passage
- computerized Wep key secret key recuperation
- Secret phrase list the executives
- [securitytrails@kali root]$ aircrack-ng
- Aircrack-ng 1.2 rc4 - (c) 2006-2015 Thomas d'otreppe
- http://www.aircrack-ng.org
- utilization: aircrack-ng [options] <.cap/.ivs file(s)>

Basic choices:
- a <amode> : power assault mode (1/Wep, 2/WpA-pSK)
- e <essid> : target determination: arrange identifier
- b <bssid> : target determination: passage's MAc
- p <nbcpu> : # of cpU to utilize (default: all cpUs)
- q : empower calm mode (no status yield)
- c <macs> : consolidate the offered Aps to a virtual one
- l <file> : compose key to record

11. Kismet Wireless

Kismet Wireless is a multi-stage free Wireless LAN analyzer, sniffer and IDS (interruption discovery framework).

It's perfect with practically any sort of remote card, utilizing it in sniffing mode enables you to work with remote systems, for example, 802.11a, 802.11b, 802.11g, and 802.11n.

Kismet Wireless runs locally in Windows, Linux and BSD working frameworks (FreeBSD, NetBSD, openBSD, and MacoS).

Fundamental highlights:
- capacity to run in detached mode
- Simple identification of Wireless customers and passages
- Remote interruption identification framework
- outputs remote encryption levels for a given Ap
- Supports channel bouncing
- System logging

12. Wireshark

Wireshark is an open source multi-organize orchestrate analyzer that runs Linux, oS X, BSD, and Windows.

It's especially useful for understanding what's going on inside your framework, which speaks to its sweeping use in government, corporate and preparing undertakings.

It works thusly as tcpdump, yet Wireshark incorporates a mind boggling graphical interface that empowers you to channel, sort out and demand got data so it requires some speculation to separate. A book based structure, called tshark, is comparable to the extent features.

principle highlights include:
- GUI-pleasing interface
- Bundle live catch and detached assessment
- Full show examination

- Gzip weight and decompression on the fly
- Full VoIp examination
- Unraveling support for Ipsec, ISAKMp, Kerberos, SNMpv3, SSL/TLS, Wep, and WpA/WpA2
- Scrutinizing get archive arrangements, for instance, tcpdump (libpcap), pcap NG, catapult DcT2000, cisco Secure IDS iplog and various others

13. John the Ripper

John the Ripper is a multi-arrange cryptography testing mechanical assembly that tackles Unix, Linux, Windows and MacoS. It licenses system officials and security penetration analyzers to dispatch creature control ambushes to test the nature of any structure mystery word. It will in general be used to test encryptions, for instance, DeS, SHA-1 and various others.

Its abilities to change mystery state unscrambling methodologies are set normally, dependent upon the recognized count.

Approved and circled under the GpL license, it's a free mechanical assembly open for any person who needs to test their mystery key security.

Guideline features include:
- Dictionary ambushes and brute power testing
- Great with most working systems and cpU models
- can run normally by using crons
- postponement and Resume decisions for any yield
- Lets you portray custom letters while building dictionary ambush records
- Grants creature control customization rules

14. THc Hydra

THc Hydra is a free hacking device approved under AGpL v3.0, extensively used by the people who need to creature control split remote check organizations.

As it reinforces up to more than 50 shows, it's maybe the best gadget for testing your mystery word security levels in a server circumstance.

It moreover offers assistance for most surely understood working structures like Windows, Linux, Free BSD, Solaris and oS X.

principal features:
- Ultrafast mystery key parting rate
- Runs on different working systems
- Ability to dispatch parallel savage power breaking ambushes
- Module-based application empowers you to incorporate custom modules
- Sponsorship for various shows, for instance, cVS, FTp, HTTp, HTTpS, HTTp-proxy, IMAp, IRc, LDAp, MS-SQL, MySQL, etc.

15. findmyhash

Written in python, findmyhash is a free open-source gadget that parts passwords using free online organizations.

It works with the going with counts: MD4, MD5, SHA1, SHA225, SHA256, SHA384, SHA512, RMD160, GoST, WHIRLpooL, LM, NTLM, MYSQL, cIScO7, JUNIpeR, LDAp_MD5, and LDAp_SHA1. It also supports multi-string assessment for snappier speed and figuring affirmation from the hash regard.

essential features include:
- Void hashes affirmation
- examines commitment from a book record
- Ability to escape novel characters
- parts single or different hashes
- Mystery key hash search on Google
- Relief and Resume decisions
- Recuperations of the results in a record

16. Rainbowcrack

Rainbowcrack is a mystery expression parting mechanical assembly available for Windows and Linux working structures.

Not under any condition like other mystery state breaking instruments, Rainbowcrack uses a period memory tradeoff estimation to part hashes close by enormous pre-prepared "rainbow tables" that help to diminish mystery word parting time.

Features include:
- Available terminal-based and GUI-pleasing interface
- Functions outstandingly with multi-focus processors
- Rainbow table age, sort, change and question
- Backing for GpU accelerating (Nvidia cUDA and AMD opencL)
- Bolster rainbow table of any hash count and char set.
- Bolster rainbow table in unrefined report plan (.rt) and littler record gathering (.rtc).

17. Metasploit Framework

Metasploit Framework is a Ruby-based stage used to make, test and execute abuses against remote hosts. It joins a full combination of security gadgets used for entrance testing, nearby a weighty terminal-based solace — called msfconsole — which empowers you to find targets, dispatch checks, misuse security flaws and accumulate each and every open datum. Available for Linux and Windows, MSF is probably one of the most predominant security looking at gadgets transparently open for the infosec promote.

What might you have the option to do with Metasploit Framework?
- Framework rundown and revelation
- evade disclosure on remote hosts
- experience headway and execution
- Work with the MFS console
- clear remote targets
- experience vulnerabilities and assemble significant data

18. Social engineering Toolkit

Available for Linux and Mac oS X, the Social engineering Toolkit (known as SeT) is an open-source python-based passage testing framework that will help you with impelling Social-engineering ambushes immediately.

Have you anytime thought about how to hack relational association accounts? everything considered, SeT has the proper reaction — it's imperative for those enthusiastic about the field of social structuring.

What kind of attacks would I have the option to dispatch with SeT?
- WiFi Ap-based ambushes: this kind of attack will occupy or get groups from customers using our WiFi arrange
- SMS and email attacks: here, SeT will endeavour to delude and create a fake email to get social accreditations
- electronic attacks: lets you clone a site page so you can drive authentic customers by DNS personifying or phishing ambushes.
- Generation of payloads (.exe): SeT will make a pernicious .exe record that, after executed, will deal the plan of the customer who taps on it

Highlighted features include:
- Speedy passageway testing
- coordination with pariah modules
- phishing attack generaToR
- Dispatch QR code attacks
- Sponsorship for power shell ambush vecToRs
- SeT Kali Security Trails

19. Hamburger

Hamburger speaks to The Browser exploitation Framework, a noteworthy passage testing gadget that relies upon program vulnerabilities and blemishes to mishandle the host.

Not under any condition like other Kali cyber security mechanical assemblies, it bases on the program side, including attacks against flexible and work region clients, letting you dismember exploitability of any Mac and Linux structure.

You'll have the choice to pick express modules dynamically to audit your program security.

Meet requirements:
- Working framework: Mac oS X 10.5.0 or higher/current Linux
- Ruby 2.3 or increasingly present
- SQLite 3.x
- Node.js at least 6 current

essential features:
- Web and solace UI
- Metasploit mix
- Detached structure
- Interprocess correspondence and abuse
- HisToRy get-together and information
- Host and framework perception
- Ability to recognize program modules

20. Yersinia

Yersinia is a security compose mechanical assembly that empowers you to perform L2 ambushes by abusing security absconds in different framework shows.

This gadget can attack switches, switches, DHcp servers and various shows. It joins an indulgent GTK GUI, ncurses-based mode, can examine from a hand craft archive, supports researching mode and offers to save results in a log record.

Reinforced compose shows:
- 802.1q and 802.1x Wireless LANs
- cisco Discovery protocol (cDp)
- Dynamic Host configuration protocol (DHcp)
- Dynamic Trunking protocol (DTp)
- Between Switch Link protocol (ISL)
- Hot Standby Router protocol (HSRp)
- Spreading over Tree protocol (STp)
- VLAN Trunking protocol (VTp)

21. DHcpig

DHcpig is a DHcp exhaustion application that will dispatch a pushed ambush to consume each and every unique Ip on the LAN.

It in like manner prevents new customers from getting Ips distributed to their pcs. Works genuinely well ambushing Linux LANs similarly as Windows 2003, 2008, etc.

In all honesty, DHcpig doesn't require any foundation, as it is a minor substance; it just requires scapy library presented on your structure, and it fuses support for ipv4 and ipv6.

What might you have the option to do with DHcpig?
- Recognize/print DHcp answers
- Recognize/print IcMp requests
- Find and make a framework guide of your neighbour's' Ips
- Sales all possible Ip addresses in a zone
- Make a circle and send DHcp requests from different MAc addresses
- Research your neighbour's MAc and Ip addresses
- Release Ips and MAc address from the DHcp server
- ARp for all neighbours on that LAN
- Knock off framework on Windows systems

22. Funk Load

Written in python, Funk Load is a notable web-stress gadget that works by impersonating a totally helpful web program. It's incredibly significant for testing web endeavours and seeing how well they react similarly as web server execution.

Funk Load allows full execution testing to help you with recognizing potential bottlenecks inside your web applications and web servers, all the while testing your application recoverability time.

essential Funk Load features include:

- Veritable web program impersonating (tallying GeT/poST/pUT/DeLeTe, DAV, treat, referrer support, etc)
- Bearing line impelled tests
- Full benchmarking reports in pDF, HTML, ReST, org-mode
- Benchmark differential relationship between's 2 results
- Test customization using a plan report
- Full help for understood servers, for instance, pHp, python, Java

23. Slow HTTp Test

Slow HTTp Test is one of the most popular web-stress applications used to dispatch DoS attacks against any HTTp server. This kind of security instrument bases on sending low-information move limit attacks to test your web-server prosperity and response times. It consolidates bits of knowledge of all of your tests and empowers you to run various sorts of ambushes, for instance,

- Apache Range Header.
- Slow Read.
- Slow HTTp poST.
- Slowloris.

essential features include:
- Saving estimations yield in HTML and cSV reports
- Setting verbose level (0-4)
- concentrating on custom number of affiliations
- Setting HTTp affiliation rate (each second)
- Go-between traffic redirection
- Slow HTTp Test

24. InundaToR

InundaToR is a multi-hung IDS shirking security instrument proposed to be obscure. By using ToR it can flood interference revelation systems (especially with Snort) causing counterfeit positives, which hide the real ambush happening out of sight t. By using SocKS delegate it can create more than 1k sham positives each minute during an attack.

The standard target of InundaToR is to keep your security bunch busy with overseeing counterfeit positives while a certifiable attack is happening.

InundaToR features and properties include:
- Multi-hung capacities
- Full SocKS support
- Anonymization-arranged
- Support of various targets
- Line based

25. t50

t50 is another web-stress testing device included with Kali Linux dissemination. It can assist you with testing how your sites, servers and systems respond under high burden normal during an assault.

It's one of only a handful barely any security instruments fit for exemplifying conventions utilizing GRe (Generic Routing encapsulation), and supports up to 14 unique conventions. The t50 bundle likewise lets you send all conventions consecutively utilizing one single SocKeT.

t50 highlights:
- DoS and DDoS assaults test system
- primary upheld conventions incorporate Tcp, UDp, IcMp, IGMp, and so forth.
- Up to 1,000,000 pps of SYN Flood if utilizing Gigabit organize
- Up to 120k pps of SYN Flood if utilizing 100Mbps system

Synopsis

Nowadays Kali Linux offers what is likely the best good hacking and invasion testing suites on the planet; because of their wide documentation, system and gadgets, starting in the infosec world isn't as hard as it was 20 years earlier; nowadays you can find pre-collected gadgets for about anything you imagine.

By executing these Kali Linux gadgets, your item association will have more ways to deal with test and construct the security of your web applications and structures — by perceiving security defects before the villains do.

chapter Seven- Basics of Networking

The defaults organize arrangement depends on DHcp to acquire an Ip address, DNS server, and passage, yet you can utilize the rigging symbol in the lower-right corner to adjust the design from various perspectives (for instance: set the MAc address, change to a static arrangement, empower or cripple Ipv6, and include extra courses). You can make profiles to spare different wired system designs and effectively switch between them. For remote systems, their settings are consequently attached to their open identifier (SSID).
Network Manager likewise handles associations by versatile broadband (Wireless Wide Area Network WWAN) and by modems utilizing point-to-point convention over ethernet (pppoe). To wrap things up, it gives coordination numerous kinds of virtual private systems (VpN) through devoted modules: SSH, openVpN, cisco's VpNc, ppTp, Strong swan. Look at the system chief * bundles; the greater part of them are not introduced as a matter of course. Note that you need the bundles suffixed with - dwarf to have the option to design them through the graphical UI.
on the command Line with Ifupdown
Then again, when you incline toward not to utilize (or don't approach) a graphical work area, you can arrange the system with the as of now introduced ifupdown bundle, which incorporates the ifup and ifdown apparatuses. These instruments read definitions from the/and so forth/organize/interfaces design record and are at the core of the/and so forth/init.d/organizing init content that arranges the system at boot time.
each system gadget oversaw by ifupdown can be reconfigured whenever with ifdown organize gadget. You would then be able to alter/and so on/organize/interfaces and bring the system back up (with the new arrangement) with ifup organize gadget.
We should investigate what we can place in ifupdown's design record. There are two fundamental mandates: auto organize gadget, which advises ifupdown to naturally arrange the system interface once it is accessible, and iface organize gadget inet/inet6 type to design a given interface.
For remote interfaces, you should have the wpasupplicant bundle (remembered for Kali of course), which gives numerous wpa-* alternatives that can be utilized in/and so forth/organize/interfaces. examine/usr/share/doc/wpasupplicant/ReADMe.Debian.gz for models and clarifications. The most widely recognized alternatives are wpa-ssid (which characterizes the name of the remote system to join) and wpa-psk (which characterizes the passphrase or the key securing the system).

While ifupdown is the recorded apparatus utilized by Debian, and keeping in mind that it is as yet the default for server or other insignificant establishments, there is a more up to date instrument worth considering: systemd-networkd. Its joining with the systemd init framework settles on it an alluring decision. It isn't explicit to Debian-based appropriations (in opposition to ifupdown) and has been intended to be little, proficient, and generally simple to arrange on the off chance that you comprehend the punctuation of systemd unit documents. This is a particularly alluring decision on the off chance that you consider NetworkManager enlarged and difficult to design.

You arrange systemd-networkd by putting .organize records into the/and so on/systemd/arrange/index. on the other hand, you can utilize/lib/systemd/organize/for bundled records or/run/systemd/arrange/for documents created at run-time. The arrangement of those records is archived in systemd.network(5). The Match segment demonstrates the system interfaces the design applies to. You can indicate the interface from numerous points of view, including by media get to control (MAc) address or gadget type. The Network segment characterizes the system setup.

In spite of the fact that systemd-networkd experiences a few restrictions, similar to the absence of coordinated help for remote systems, you can depend on a prior outer wpa_supplicant design for remote help. Be that as it may, it is especially helpful in holders and virtual machines and was initially created for situations in which a compartment's system arrangement relied upon its host's system design. In this situation, systemd-networkd makes it simpler to oversee the two sides in a steady way while as yet supporting a wide range of virtual system gadgets that you may require in this kind of situation (see systemd.netdev(5)).

chapter eight- proxy and proxy chains

By and by these days, pretty much all that we do on web is pursued. Whoever is doing the accompanying - it may be Google following our online missions, webpage visits, and email or it may be the National Security Agency (NSA) ordering all our each online development is being recorded, documented, and a short time later burrowed for their bit of leeway. The run of the mill customers and security experts everyone needs to perceive how to keep this following and remain commonly baffling on the web and limit this ubiquitous surveillance.

In this ordered theoretical we look how we can investigate the World Wide Web anonymously (or as close as we can get) and safely using four procedures:

1.The onion Router

2.Intermediary servers

3.Virtual private Networks

4. private encoded email

No one strategy makes sure to keep our activities safe from prying eyes and given adequate chance and resources, anything can be pursued. At any rate we can use all methods together; this will make the tracker's action for all intents and purposes incomprehensible.

We should start; finally we talk about at a critical level a bit of the habits in which our activity on the web is pursued. We won't go into every after procedure, or into an inordinate measure of bits of knowledge concerning only a solitary technique, as that would be past the degree of this post. Actually such a talk could take up an entire book separately.

To begin with, our Ip address remembers us as we cross the web. Data send from our machine is ordinarily marked with our Ip address, making our activities easy to pursue. Second, Google and other email organizations will examine our email, scanning for watchwords to even more profitably serve the advancements. Notwithstanding the way that there are a great deal logically present day methods that are certainly extra time and resource focused, these are the ones we endeavour to foresee in this post. We should start by researching how Ip address part with us on the web.

exactly when we send a data package over the web, it contains the Ip address of the source and objective for the data. Thusly, the pack knows where it is going and where to re-establish the response. each pack hops through various web switches until it finds its objective and short time later bobs back to the sender. For general web surfing each ricochet is a switch the packages experiences to get to its objective, anyway regularly any group will find its way to the objective in less than 15 bounces.

As the group crosses the web, anyone catching the bundle can see who sent it, where it has been, and it's going. This is one way destinations can tell who we are when appear and log us in normally, and it's moreover how someone can pursue where we have been on the web.

1. ToR -- The onion Router

In the year 1990, the US office of Naval Research (oNR) set out to build up a strategy for namelessly exploring the web for undercover work reason. The arrangement was to set up a system of switches that was isolated from the web switches, that could encode the traffic, and that just put away decoded Ip address of our past switch.

That implies every other switch address en route was encoded. The thought was that anybody watching the traffic couldn't decide the root or goal of the information. This examination became known as "The onion Router (ToR) project" In 2002, it is accessible for everybody to utilize protected and unknown route on the web.

How ToR Works

Bundles send over ToR are not sent over the customary switches so intently checked by such a significant number of rather are sent over a system of over 7000+ switches far and wide, unique gratitude to volunteers who enable their pcs to be utilized by ToR. over utilizing an absolutely isolated switch organize, ToR scrambles the information, goal, and sender Ip address of every bundle. At each bounce, the data is encoded and afterward unscrambled by the following jump when it is gotten. Thusly, every parcel contains data about just the past bounce along the way and not the Ip address of the traffic. In the event that somebody catches the traffic, they can see just the Ip address of past jump, and the site proprieToR can see just the Ip address of the last switch that send the traffic. Along these lines ToR guarantee relative obscurity over the web.

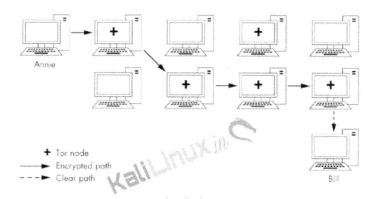

How ToR uses encrypted traffic data

To enable the use of ToR, the browser needs to be installed from the website: https://www.ToRproject.org/download/

Download page of ToR

ToR can be downloaded as per the operating System. In the case of Kali Linux, the "extract Here" option is to be clicked.

To open the ToR browser folder, we double click on it.

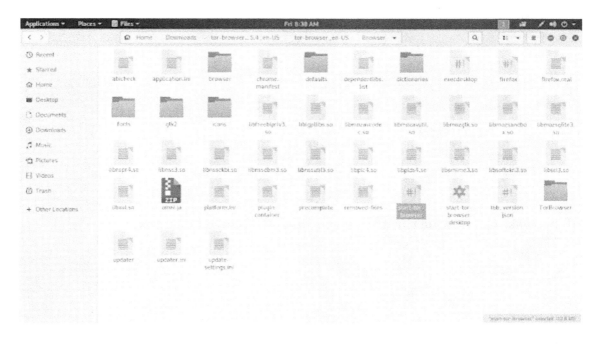

This file will be opened in text ediToR and root will be searched for by using ctrl+F key.

```
            -buttons GTK_STOCK_OK \
            -default OK \
            $complain_message
        if [ $? -ne 127 ]; thenF
            return
        fi
}

if [ id -u -eq 0 ]; then
        complain                                           root
        exit 1
fi

if ! grep -q                          /proc/cpuinfo; then
        complain
        exit 1
fi

tbb_usage () {
    printf
    printf
    printf
```

```
                return
        fi
}
#if [ "`id -u`" -eq 0 ]; then
#       complain "The Tor Browser Bundle should not be run as root.  Exiting."
#       exit 1
#fi

if ! grep -q ^flags.*:.* sse2 /proc/cpuinfo; then
        complain "Tor Browser requires a CPU with SSE2 support.  Exiting."
        exit 1
fi
```

The ToR browser can now be run after performing the above functions:

Next, you open up the terminal and type in the desired command.

```
./start-ToR-browser.desktop
```

After clicking on connect, the browser opens up this way:

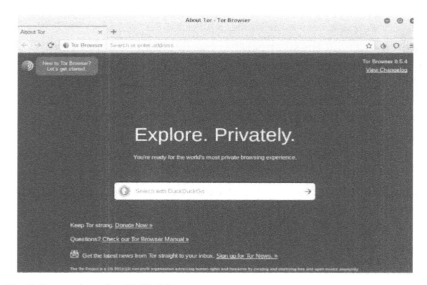

ToR Browser in Kali Linux

It would appear that any old web program. By utilizing this program, we will explore the web through a different arrangement of switches and will have the option to visit without being followed by anybody. Lamentably, the exchange off is that by means of the ToR program can be bit more slow, in light of the fact that there are not such huge numbers of switches, the data transfer capacity is constrained in ToR arrange.

What's more, to being fit for getting to about any site on the customary web, the ToR program is equipped for getting to the dull web. The sites that make up the dim web requires namelessness, hence they permit get to just through the ToR program, and dull sites have address finishing with .onion for their top level space (TLD). The dim web is scandalous for criminal behavior, however a few quantities of real administrations are likewise accessible in dull web. A few words for alert, anyway while getting to the dim web, we may go over material that many will discover hostile. See how we can have our own .onion dim web for nothing by clicking here.

Security concerns

The insight and spy administrations of the United States and different countries consider the ToR organize as a danger to national security, accepting such an unknown system empowers remote governments and fear based oppressors to convey without being viewed. Subsequently, some strong, driven research ventures are attempting to break the obscurity of ToR.

ToR's namelessness has been broken before by these specialists and will probably break once more. The NSA, as one occurrence, runs it's own ToR switches, implies that our traffic might be crossing the NSA's switches when we use ToR. on the off chance that our traffic is leaving the NSA's switches that is far more terrible, in light of the fact that the leave switch consistently knows our goal, however this will be difficult to follow us. The NSA additionally has a technique known as traffic relationship, which includes searching for designs in approaching and active rush hour gridlock that has had the option to break ToR's secrecy. In spite of the fact that these endeavours to break ToR won't influence ToR's adequacy at darkening our character for business administrations, for example, Google, they may restrain the program's viability in keeping us unknown from spy organizations.

2. proxy Servers

Another procedure for accomplishing secrecy on the web is to utilize intermediaries, which are middle of the road frameworks that client associates with an intermediary, and the traffic is given the Ip address of the intermediary before it's passed on. We can see the accompanying picture.

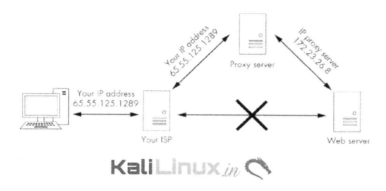

At the point when the traffic comes back from the goals the intermediary sends the traffic back to the source. Along these lines, traffic seems to originate from the intermediary and not our Ip address.

clearly, the intermediary servers likely log our traffic, yet a research ToR would need to get a subpoena or court order to acquire our logs. To make our traffic considerably harder to follow, we can utilize more than one intermediary, this procedure known as intermediary chain. Kali Linux has a delightful intermediary device called proxy chains that can set up to darken our traffic.

Security concerns

A note on intermediary security makes certain to pick your intermediaries shrewdly. proxy chains are just in the same class as the proxy we use. In the event that we are resolved to staying mysterious, we ought not to utilize free proxy. Specialists utilize paid proxy that can be trusted. Indeed the free proxies are likely selling our Ip address and perusing history. Bruce Schneier a well known security master said "If something is free, you're not the client; you are the item." at the end of the day any free item is likely assembling our information and selling it. For what other reason would they offer an intermediary for nothing?

In spite of the fact that, the Ip address of our traffic leaving the proxy will be unknown, there are different ways for observation organizations to distinguish us. For example the proprietor or law authorization offices with purview, may present our character to ensure their business. It's imperative to know about the confinements of proxies as a wellspring of namelessness.

3. Virtual private Networks (VpN)

Utilizing a virtual private system (VpN) can be compelling approach to keep our web traffic moderately unknown and secure. A VpN is utilized to interface with a delegate web gadget, for example, a switch that sends our traffic to it's definitive goal labeled with the Ip address of the switch.

Utilizing a VpN can unquestionably upgrade our security and protection, yet it isn't assurance of namelessness. The web gadget we interface with must record our Ip address can reveal data about us.

The excellence of VpN is that they are basic and simple to work with. We can open a record with a VpN supplier and afterward flawlessly associate with the VpN each time we sign on to our pc. We can utilize our program as common to explore the web, however it will appear to anybody watching that our traffic is originating from the Ip address and area of the web VpN gadget, not our own. What's more, all traffic among us and the VpN gadgets is encoded, so even our internet service can't see our traffic. In addition to other things, a VpN can be successful in dodging government controlled substance and data blue pencils. For example, if our national government confines our entrance to sites with a specific political message, we can almost certainly utilize a VpN based outside our nation so as to get to that substance. A few media organizations like Netflix, Hulu and HBo limit access to their substance to Ip address starting from their own nation. Utilizing a VpN situated in a country that those administrations permit can frequently get us around to cNeT are following:

- Ip Vanish
- Nord VpN
- express VpN
- cyber ghost
- Golden frog VpN
- private Internet Access
- pure VpN
- ToR Guard
- Buffered VpN

A large portion of these VpN administrations charge $50 - $100 every year, and numerous offers a free multi day trail. To discover increasingly about how to set up a VpN, pick one from the rundown and visit the site. We should discover download, establishment and utilizations directions that are very simple to pursue.

The quality of a VpN is that all our traffic is scrambled when it leaves our pc/portable, consequently ensuring us against snooping, and our Ip address is shrouded by the VpN Ip address when we visit a site. Likewise with an intermediary server, the administrator of the VpN has our starting Ip address (else they couldn't send our traffic back to us). In the event that they are compelled by secret activities organizations or law requirement, they may surrender our personality. one approach to avert that is to utilize just VpN's that vowed not to store or log any of this data (and we trust they are being honest). Thusly, on the off chance that somebody demand that the VpN specialist co-op to check their information of clients, there is no information.

4. encrypted e-mail

Free commercial email services like Gmail, Yahoo!, outlook, and Hotmail are free for a reason. They are vehicles for tracking our interests and serving their ads. As Mentioned earlier, if a service is free then we are the product, not the customer. In addition, the servers of the email provider have access to the unencrypted content of our emails, even if we're using HTTpS.
one way to prevent eavesdropping on our email is to use encrypted email.
proton Mail, encrypts our email from end to end or browser to browser. This means that our email is encrypted on proton Mail servers. even the proton Mail owners can't read our emails.

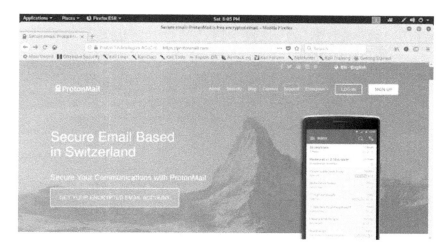
proton Mail Homepage

proton Mail was established by a gathering of youthful researchers at the ceRN super collider office in Switzerland. The Swiss have a major and storied history of securing privileged insights (recollect the Swiss ledgers), and proton Mail's servers are situated in the european Union, which has a lot stricter laws with respect to the sharing of individual information at that point does the US. proton Mail doesn't charge for a fundamental record yet offers premium records at an ostensible cost. It is significant for a few or the entirety of the email not to be encoded. check the proton Mail bolster information base for full subtleties.

conclusion

We are continually being shrivelled by business firms and national knowledge organizations. To keep our information and web voyages secure, we have to actualize at any rate one of the safety efforts talked about in this post.
By applying them in mix we can limit our impression on the web and keep our information significantly more secure. That's it in a nutshell. Be secure and help companions to be secure by shearing this via web-based networking media.

chapter Nine- Virtual private Networks

VpNs are utilized to give remote corporate representatives, gig economy independent laborers and business explorers with access to programming applications facilitated on exclusive systems. To access a confined asset through a VpN, the client must be approved to utilize the VpN application and give at least one confirmation factors, for example, a secret phrase, security token or biometric information.

VpN applications are regularly utilized by people who need to secure information transmissions on their cell phones or visit sites that are topographically limited. Secure access to a confined system or site through a portable VpN ought not be mistaken for private perusing, in any case. private perusing doesn't include encryption; it is basically a discretionary program setting that anticipates recognizable client information, for example, treats, from being gathered and sent to an outsider server.

How a VpN functions

At its most fundamental level, VpN burrowing makes a point-to-point association that can't be gotten to by unapproved clients. To really make the VpN burrow, the endpoint gadget should be running a VpN customer (programming application) locally or in the cloud. The VpN customer runs out of sight and isn't recognizable to the end client except if there are execution issues.

The exhibition of a VpN can be influenced by an assortment of elements, among them the speed of clients' web associations, the kinds of conventions a network access supplier may utilize and the sort of encryption the VpN employments. In the endeavor, execution can likewise be influenced by low quality of administration (QoS) outside the control of an association's data innovation (IT) office.

VpN conventions

VpN conventions guarantee a proper degree of security to associated frameworks when the hidden system foundation alone can't give it. There are a few distinct conventions used to verify and scramble clients and corporate information. They include:
- Ip security (Ipsec)
- Secure Sockets Layer (SSL) and Transport Layer Security (TLS)
- point-To-point Tunneling protocol (ppTp)
- Layer 2 Tunneling protocol (L2Tp)
- openVpN

Kinds of VpNs

System overseers have a few alternatives with regards to sending a VpN. They include:

Remote access VpN

Remote access VpN customers associate with a VpN passage server on the association's system. The door requires the gadget to validate its personality before allowing access to inward system assets, for example, record servers, printers and intranets. This sort of VpN generally depends on either Ip Security (Ipsec) or Secure Sockets Layer (SSL) to verify the association.

Site-to-site VpN

conversely, a site-to-site VpN utilizes a door gadget to interface a whole system in one area to a system in another area. end-hub gadgets in the remote area needn't bother with VpN customers in light of the fact that the entryway handles the association. Most website to-webpage VpNs associating over the web use Ipsec. It is likewise regular for them to utilize transporter MpLS mists instead of the open web as the vehicle for website to-webpage VpNs. Here, as well, it is conceivable to have either Layer 3 network (MpLS Ip VpN) or Layer 2 (virtual private LAN administration) stumbling into the base vehicle.

portable VpN

In a portable VpN, a VpN server still sits at the edge of the organization arrange, empowering secure burrowed access by validated, approved VpN customers. Versatile VpN burrows are not attached to physical Ip addresses, notwithstanding. Rather, each passage is bound to a sensible Ip address. That intelligent Ip address adheres to the cell phone regardless of where it might wander. A powerful versatile VpN gives ceaseless help to clients and can consistently switch crosswise over access innovations and different open and private systems.

equipment VpN

equipment VpNs offer various points of interest over the product based VpN. Notwithstanding upgraded security, equipment VpNs can give load adjusting to deal with enormous customer loads. organization is overseen through a Web program interface. An equipment VpN is more costly than a product VpN. on account of the cost, equipment VpNs are a more reasonable choice for huge organizations than for independent companies or branch workplaces. A few merchants, including Irish seller InvizBox, offer gadgets that can work as equipment VpNs.

VpN machine

A VpN machine, otherwise called a VpN passage apparatus, is a system gadget outfitted with upgraded security highlights. otherwise called a SSL (Secure Sockets Layer) VpN machine, it is essentially a switch that gives insurance, approval, confirmation and encryption for VpNs.

Dynamic multipoint virtual private system (DMVpN)

A dynamic multipoint virtual private system (DMVpN) is a safe system that trades information between locales without expecting to go traffic through an association's headquarter virtual private system (VpN) server or switch. A DMVpN basically makes a work VpN administration that sudden spikes in demand for VpN switches and firewall concentrators. every remote site has a switch arranged to associate with the organization's home office VpN gadget (centre), giving access to the assets accessible. At the point when two spokes are required to trade information between one another - for a VoIp phone call, for instance - the spoke will contact the centre point, acquire the essential data about the opposite end, and make a dynamic Ipsec VpN burrow straightforwardly between them.

VpN Reconnect

VpN Reconnect is an element of Windows 7 and Windows Server 2008 R2 that enables a virtual private system association with stay open during a short interference of Internet administration. As a rule, when a registering gadget utilizing a VpN association drops its Internet association, the end client needs to physically reconnect to the VpN. VpN Reconnect keeps the VpN burrow open for a configurable measure of time so when Internet administration is re-established, the VpN association is naturally re-established also. The element was intended to improve ease of use for portable representatives.

Security constraints of a virtual private system clarified

Any gadget that gets to a secluded system through a VpN presents a danger of bringing malware to that system condition except if there is a prerequisite in the VpN association procedure to surveys the condition of the interfacing gadget. Without an examination to decide if the interfacing gadget agrees to an association's security arrangements, assailants with taken certifications can get to organize assets, including switches and switches.

Security specialists suggest that system overseers consider including programming characterized edge (SDp) segments to their VpN foundation so as to diminish potential assault surfaces. The expansion of SDp programming enables medium and huge associations to utilize a zero trust model for access to both on-premises and cloud organize situations.

chapter Ten- Installing VpN on Kali Linux

Installing VpN on Kali Linux
VpN on Kali Linux is odd enough not introduced and empowered naturally which leaves you with a turned gray out VpN alternative board and a fairly troublesome, or possibly a not straight advance, set-up process on the off chance that you don't have the foggiest idea how to introduce VpN. VpN represents Virtual private Network and broadens your private system over the web which will shroud your Ip address, sidestep restriction and encode your system traffic. In this instructional exercise we will introduce the important bundles and arrangement the well known Golden Frog VyprVpN administration in Kali Linux.
I'm utilizing VyprVpN from Golden Frog as VpN administration for two or three months now on open remote systems and in outside nations for instance. Their VpN administration is quick, solid and there are numerous servers/nations to look over (50+ servers and 200,000 Ip addresses). There's an application for all stages, including Ios, Android, Windows, Mac and a VyprVpN switch application to verify your whole home system. Brilliant Frog professes to not keep logs for their VpN administrations and they have incredible applications accessible for overseeing VpN associations.
Why use VpN?
There are a few reasons why you would need to utilize a VpN administration:
- VpN shrouds your Ip address and area so you will be unknown.
- Maintain a strategic distance from web oversight, firewalls and access area confined substance.
- Scramble your system traffic (on open Wifi for instance).
- To conceal your personality.

Note that web indexes and stage can in any case remember you dependent on treats or logins for instance.
Stage 1: enabling VpN on Kali Linux
Naturally the VpN area is turned gray out on Kali Linux. You can pursue my guide on fixing VpN turned gray out issue (with screengrabs) or simply duplicate glue the directions from underneath:
There's two variations on the directions I've utilized, the first empowers a wide range of VpN and ppTp mumbo-jumbo's so you don't need to work your way through it later.
Stage 2: Download and concentrate openvpn certs from pIA
Download and concentrate the openvpn.zip record containing ca.crt in the right index:

```
root@kali:~# wget https://www.privateinternetaccess.com/openvpn/openvpn.zip
--2015-02-27 13:14:14--
https://www.privateinternetaccess.com/openvpn/openvpn.zip
Resolving www.privateinternetaccess.com (www.privateinternetaccess.com)...
23.215.245.45
```

```
connecting to www.privateinternetaccess.com (www.privateinternetaccess.com)|
23.215.245.45|:443... connected.
HTTp request sent, awaiting response... 200 oK
Length: 8242 (8.0K) [application/zip]
Saving to: `openvpn.zip'
100%[======================================>] 8,242  --.-K/s   in 0s
2015-02-27 13:14:15 (149 MB/s) - `openvpn.zip' saved [8242/8242]
root@kali:~#
root@kali:~# unzip -q openvpn.zip -d /etc/openvpn
```

Stage 3: configure Network Manager to utilize pIA VpN
Go to Network Manager > edit connections

change to VpN Tab. **VpN> Add**

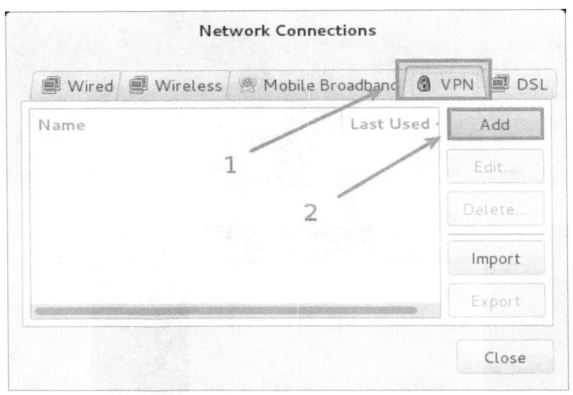

click [**ADD +**] click the drop down menu, and set the type as **openVpN**.
click [**create**]

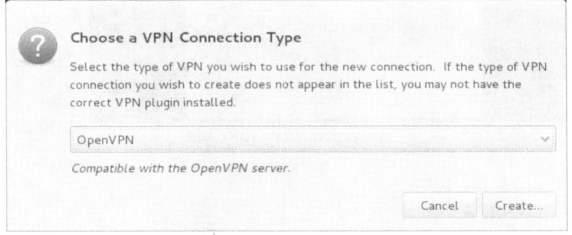

Go to "**VpN**" and fill up the following details".
- **connection name:** privateInternetAccess VpN
- **Gateway:** us-east.privateinternetaccess.com [**choose Gateway's from the list below]
- **Username:** pIA Username
- **password:** pIA password
- **cA certificate:** Browse to /etc/openvpn and select ca.crt

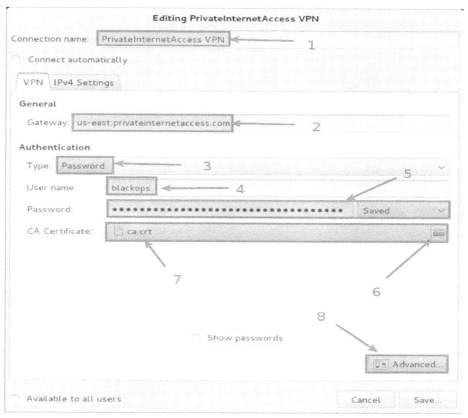

- click [**Advanced**]: check the box next to "**Use LZo data compression**"
- click [**oK**], [**Save**] and then [**close**].

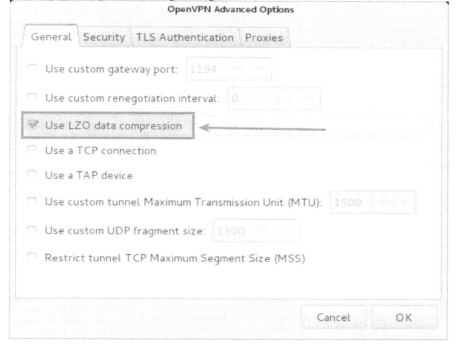

As for Gateways, choose on the following depending on your location:

chapter eleven- Securing and monitoring Kali Linux

As you use Kali Linux for progressively delicate and more prominent work, you will probably need to take the security of your establishment all the more truly. In this section, we will initially talk about security arrangements, featuring different focuses to think about when characterizing such an approach, and sketching out a portion of the dangers to your framework and to you as a security proficient. We will likewise talk about safety efforts for workstation and work area frameworks and spotlight on firewalls and parcel sifting. At long last, we will examine observing devices and procedures and tell you the best way to best execute them to distinguish potential dangers to your framework.

The security policy

It is unfeasible to examine security in general terms since the thought speaks to an immense scope of ideas, devices, and systems, none of which apply all around. picking among them requires a exact thought of what your objectives are. Verifying a framework begins with addressing a couple of inquiries and hurrying fast into actualizing a subjective arrangement of devices risks concentrating on inappropriate parts of security.

It is typically best to decide a particular objective. A decent way to deal with assistance with that assurance begins with the accompanying inquiries:

• What are you attempting to ensure? The security strategy will be distinctive relying upon whether you need to secure pcs or information. In the last case, you additionally need to know which information.

• What are you attempting to secure against? Is it spillage of classified information? coincidental information misfortune? Income misfortune brought about by disturbance of administration?

• Also, who are you attempting to ensure against? Safety efforts will be very unique for guarding against a grammatical mistake by an ordinary client of the framework as opposed to ensuring against a decided outer assailant gathering.

The expression "chance" is generally used to allude all in all to these three components: what to ensure, what ought to be anticipated, and who may get this going. Demonstrating the hazard requires answers to these three inquiries. From this hazard model, a security approach can be built and the strategy can be actualized with solid activities.

Additional limitations are likewise worth considering as they can confine the scope of accessible arrangements. How far would you say you will go to verify a framework? This inquiry majorly affects which arrangement to actualize. over and over again, the appropriate response is just characterized as far as fiscal costs, but different components ought to likewise be considered, for example, the measure of burden forced on framework clients or execution debasement.

When the hazard has been demonstrated, you can begin considering planning a genuine security approach. There are limits that can become an integral facToR when choosing the degree of security assurances to receive. on one hand, it tends to be incredibly easy to give fundamental framework security. For example, if the framework to be ensured just contains a recycled pc, the sole utilization of which is to include a couple of numbers by the day's end, choosing not to do anything extraordinary to ensure it would be very sensible. The inherent estimation of the framework is low and the estimation of the information are zero since they are not put away on the pc. A potential aggressor penetrating this framework would just increase a number cruncher. The expense of verifying such a framework would presumably be more prominent than the expense of a rupture. At the opposite finish of the range, you should secure the classification of mystery information in the most far reaching way that could be available, besting some other thought. For this situation, a fitting reaction would be the all out pulverization of the information (safely eradicating the documents, destroying of the hard circles to bits, at that point dissolving these bits in corrosive, etc). on the off chance that there is an extra prerequisite that information must be kept coming up for sometime later (in spite of the fact that not really promptly accessible), also, whenever cost still isn't a facToR, at that point a beginning stage would sToRe the information on iridium–platinum compound plates put away in bomb-evidence shelters under different mountains on the planet, every one of which being (obviously) both totally mystery and watched by whole armed forces.

extraordinary however these models may appear, they would by the by be a sufficient reaction to certain characterized dangers, to the extent that they are the result of a point of view that considers the objectives to reach and the limitations to satisfy. When originating from a contemplated choice, no security strategy is more, or less, decent than some other. Returning to an increasingly average case, a data framework can be portioned into predictable and for the most part free subsystems. every subsystem will have its own prerequisites and limitations, thus the hazard evaluation and the structure of the security approach ought to be embraced independently for each. A decent guideline to remember is that a little assault surface is simpler to safeguard than a huge one. The system association ought to likewise be structured appropriately: the delicate administrations ought to be focused on few machines, and these machines should just be open through a negligible number of courses or registration. The rationale is direct: it is simpler to verify these checkpoints than to verify all the delicate machines against the total of the outside world. It is now that the value of system sifting (counting by firewalls) gets obvious. This separating can be executed with committed equipment however a less difficult and increasingly adaptable arrangement is to utilize a product firewall, for example, the one coordinated in the Linux part.

<u>Security measures on a server</u>

on the off chance that you run Kali Linux on a freely open server, you probably need to verify arrange benefits by changing any default passwords that may be designed, "Verifying Network Services" and perhaps at the same time by confining their entrance with a firewall.

In the event that you hand out client accounts either straightforwardly on the server or on one of the administrations, you need to guarantee that you set solid passwords (they should oppose savage power assaults). Simultaneously, you may need to arrangement fail2ban, which will make it a lot harder to beast power passwords over the system (by separating ceaselessly Ip tends to that surpass a farthest point of fizzled login endeavors). Introduce fail2ban with well-suited update pursued by well-suited introduce fail2ban.

In the event that you run web administrations, you likely need to have them over HTTpS to counteract arrange middle people from sniffing your traffic (which may incorporate validation treats).

Security measures on a laptop

The pc of an infiltration analyzer isn't dependent upon indistinguishable dangers from an open server: for example, you are more averse to be dependent upon irregular outputs from content kiddies and in any event, when you will be, you presumably won't have any system administrations empowered. Genuine hazard regularly emerges when you make a trip starting with one client then onto the next. For instance, your workstation could be taken while voyaging or seized by customs. That is the reason you probably need to utilize full circle encryption, and perhaps at the same time arrangement the "nuke" the information that you have gathered during your commitment are private and require the most extreme assurance.

You may likewise require firewall rules yet not for a similar reason as on the server. You should preclude all outbound traffic with the exception of the traffic created by your VpN get to. This is implied as a wellbeing net, so when the VpN is down, you quickly notice it (rather than falling back to the nearby system get to). That way, you try not to reveal the Ip locations of your clients when you peruse the web or do other on the web exercises. Also, in the event that you are playing out a neighborhood inside commitment, it is ideal to stay in control of the entirety of your action to decrease the commotion you make on the system, which can caution the client and their barrier frameworks.

Security of network devices

When all is said in done, it is a smart thought to debilitate administrations that you don't utilize. Kali makes it simple since most system administrations are debilitated as a matter of course. For whatever length of time that administrations stay debilitated, they don't represent any security risk. Be that as it may, you should be cautious when you empower them on the grounds that:

• there is no firewall naturally, so on the off chance that they tune in on all system interfaces, they are adequately freely accessible.

• a few administrations have no verification qualifications and let you set them on first use; othershave default (and in this way generally known) certifications preset. Try to (re)set any secret key to something that solitary you know.

• numerous administrations run as root with full overseer benefits, so the outcomes of unapproved get to or a security rupture are in this way typically extreme.

Firewall and packet filtering

A firewall is a bit of pc gear with equipment, programming, or both that parses the approaching or active system bundles (coming to or leaving from a nearby system) and just lets through those coordinating certain predefined conditions.

A separating system entryway is a kind of firewall that secures a whole system. It is normally introduced on a committed machine designed as a passage for the system with the goal that it can parse all bundles that go all through the system. Then again, a nearby firewall is a product administration that sudden spikes in demand for one specific machine so as to channel or restrain access to certain administrations on that machine, or conceivably to avert active associations by maverick programming that a client could, energetically or not, have introduced.

The Linux piece inserts the netfilter firewall. There is no turn-key answer for designing any firewall since system and client necessities vary. Notwithstanding, you can control netfilter from client space with the iptables and ip6tables directions. The distinction between these two directions is that the previous works for Ipv4 systems, though the last deals with Ipv6. Since both system convention stacks will most likely be around for a long time, the two devices should be utilized in parallel.

You can likewise utilize the great GUI-based fwbuilder instrument, which gives a graphical portrayal of the separating rules. Anyway you choose to arrange it, netfilter Linux's firewall execution, so how about we investigate how it functions.

Netfilter utilizes four particular tables, which sToRe rules directing three sorts of activities on parcels:
- GJMUFS concerns sifting rules (tolerating, won't, or disregarding a parcel);
- oBU (Network Address Translation) concerns interpretation of source or goal addresses also, ports of bundles;
- NBoHMF concerns different changes to the Ip bundles (counting the ToS—Type of Service—field furthermore, alternatives);
- SBX permits other manual adjustments on bundles before they arrive at the association following framework. each table contains arrangements of rules called chains. The firewall utilizes standard chains to deal with parcels in view of predefined conditions. The overseer can make different chains, which will as it were be utilized when alluded by one of the standard chains (either legitimately or in a roundabout way).

The GJMUFS table has three standard chains:
- */165: concerns bundles whose goal is simply the firewall;
- 065165: concerns bundles radiated by the firewall;
- '038"3%: concerns bundles going through the firewall (which is neither their source nor their goal).

The oBU table additionally has three standard chains:
- 13&3065*/(: to alter bundles when they show up;
- 10453065*/(: to alter bundles when they are all set on their way;
- 065165: to alter bundles produced by the firewall itself.

chapter Twelve- Debian package Management

After the stray pieces of Linux, the opportunity has arrived to pick up capability with the group the administrators course of action of a Debian-based scattering. In such scatterings, including Kali, the Debian pack is the legitimate technique to make programming available to end-customers.

Understanding the pack the board structure will give you a great deal of comprehension into how Kali is composed, engage you to even more effectively research issues, and help you quickly discover help and documentation for the wide group of gadgets and utilities associated with Kali Linux.

In this part, we will exhibit the Debian pack the officials system and present dpkg and the ApT suite of instruments. one of the fundamental characteristics of Kali Linux lies in the versatility of its pack the officials system, which utilize these contraptions to give close steady foundation, updates, removal, and control of utilization programming, and even of the base working structure itself. It is significant that you perceive how this system endeavours to exploit Kali and streamline your undertakings. The hours of troublesome gatherings, terrible updates, exploring gcc, make, and configuration issues are ancient history, in any case, the amount of available applications has exploded besides, you need to grasp the instruments planned to abuse them. This is moreover a fundamental mastery considering the way that there are different security instruments that, due to approving or various issues, can't be associated with Kali anyway have Debian groups open for download. It is huge that you realize the best technique to process and present these groups and how they influence the system, especially when things do whatever it takes not to go exactly as expected.

We will begin with some basic audits of ApT, depict the structure and substance of combined and source packs, examine some basic mechanical assemblies and circumstances, and thereafter tunnel further to help you wring every ounce of utility from this heavenly group system and suite of gadgets.

A Debian group is a pressed record of an item application. A twofold group (a .deb record) contains reports that can be clearly used, (for instance, tasks or documentation), while a source pack contains the source code for the item and the rules required for building a twofold group. A Debian pack contains the application's records similarly as other metadata including the names of the conditions the application needs, similarly as substance that engage the execution of headings at different stages in the group's lifecycle (foundation, ejection, and upgrades).The dpkg instrument was proposed to process and present .deb packs, yet in case it encountered an unsatisfied dependence (like a missing library) that would prevent the group from presenting, dpkg would fundamentally list the missing dependence, since it had no care or understood basis to find or process the packs that may satisfy those conditions. The Advanced package Tool (ApT), tallying appropriate and capable get, were proposed to address these shortcomings and could thusly resolve these issues. We will talk about both dpkg and the ApT instruments in this chapter. The base bearing for dealing with Debian packages on the system is dpkg, which performs foundation or assessment of .deb groups and their substance. In any case, dpkg has only a fragmentary point of view on the Debian universe: it perceives what is presented on the system and whatever you give on the request line, yet stays ignorant of the other open packs. everything thought of it as, will crash and burn if a dependence isn't met. Skilled keeps an eye on the obstructions. capable is a great deal of instruments that help direct Debian packs, or applications on your Debian structure. You can use ApT to present and empty applications, update packages, and even overhaul your entire system. The charm of ApT lies in the manner that it is a completed group the board structure that won't simply present or oust a pack, anyway will consider the necessities and states of the packaged application (and even their requirements and conditions) and attempt to satisfy them therefore. Adroit relies upon dpkg anyway ApT complexities from dpkg, as the past presents the latest group from an online source and endeavours to decide conditions while dpkg presents a pack arranged on your close by structure and doesn't subsequently resolve conditions. If you have been around adequately long to review fusing programs with gcc (even with the assistance of utilities, for instance, make and orchestrate), you likely review that it was an agonizing method, especially if the application had a couple of conditions. By translating the various cautions and botch messages, you may have the choice to make sense of which some segment of the code was crashing and burning and consistently that mistake was a direct result of a missing library or other dependence. You would then locate that missing library or dependence, right it, and endeavor again. By then, if you were lucky, the join would complete, yet habitually the build would tumble again, protesting about another destroyed dependence. capable was proposed to help facilitate that issue, accumulate program essentials and conditions, additionally, resolve them. This value works out-of-the-holder on Kali Linux, yet it isn't verify. It is critical that you perceive how Debian and Kali's packaging system capacities since you should present groups, update programming, or explore issues with packs. You will use capable in your ordinary work with Kali Linux and in this area, we will familiarize you with ApT what's more, reveal to you the most ideal approach to present, clear, upgrade, and administer packages, and even show you the most ideal approach to move packages between different Linux scatterings. We will in like manner talk about graphical contraptions that impact ApT, disclose to you the most ideal approach to favour the believability of groups, and plunge into the possibility of a moving dispersal, a strategy that conveys step by step updates to your Kali system.

Before we dig in and reveal to you the most ideal approach to use dpkg and ApT to present and supervise groups, it is noteworthy that we dive into a part of the inner tasks of ApT and discussion about some expressing incorporating it.

chapter Thirteen- Advanced Usage

Kali has been filled in as a significantly specific and flexible invasion testing framework and considers some truly moved customization and use. customizations can happen at various levels, beginning at the source code level. The wellsprings of all Kali packs are openly available. In this part, we will show how you can recuperate packs, change them, and build your own special adjusted packages out of them. The Linux part is somewhat an extraordinary case and in that limit, where we will discuss where to find sources, how to structure the piece produce, in conclusion how to arrange it and how to manufacture the related piece groups. The second level of customization is gathering live ISo pictures. We will show how the live-structure contraption offers a ton of catches and course of action decisions to change the consequent ISo picture, including the probability to use custom Debian packages rather than the groups open on mirrors. We will similarly discuss how you can make a determined live ISo manufactured onto a USB key that will secure records and working system changes between reboots.

Adjusting Kali groups is typically a task for Kali supporters and architects: they update packs with new upstream structures, they change the default course of action for a predominant blend in the dissemination, or they fix bugs reported by customers. Notwithstanding, you may have unequivocal needs not fulfilled by the official packages and acknowledging how to build a balanced group would in this manner have the option to be really noteworthy. You may inquire as to why you need to sit around with the group in any way shape or form. everything considered, if you have to alter a touch of programming, you can for the most part grab its source code (generally with git) and run the changed structure direct from the source checkout. This is fine when it is possible and when you use your home vault consequently, yet if your application requires a structure wide game plan (for example, with a make present advance) by then it will sully your report system with records darken to dpkg and will after a short time make gives that can't be gotten by pack conditions. In addition, with real packages you will have the choice to share your movements and pass on them on different pcs impressively more successfully or return the movements in the wake of having discovered that they were not working similarly as you trusted. So when may you have to alter a group? We should research two or three models. In any case, we will expect that you are a staggering customer of SeT and you saw another upstream release yet the Kali architects are generally involved for a gathering and you have to give it a shot immediately. You have to revive the group yourself. For another circumstance, we will expect that you are endeavouring to get your MIFARe NFc card working and you have to redo "lib free fare" to engage research messages to have critical data to give in a bug report that you are starting at now arranging. In a last case, we will acknowledge that the "pyrit" program crashes and burns with a mysterious screw up message. After a web search, you find a present that you would like to fix your anxiety in the upstream GitHub vault and you have to patch up the group with this fix applied.

We will encounter every single one of those models in the going with territories. We will endeavour to summarize the explanations with the objective that you can all the more probable apply the rules to various cases yet it is hard to cover all conditions that you may understanding. In case you hit issues, apply your best judgment to find an answer or go search for help on the most appropriate social affairs.

Whatever change you have to make, the general technique is reliably the proportional: get the source pack, separate it, reveal your enhancements, by then manufacture the group. Regardless, for every movement, there are routinely unique mechanical assemblies that can manage the endeavour. We picked the most appropriate and most surely understood instruments, yet our review isn't intensive.

Since the Linux piece sources are open as a pack, you can recoup them by presenting the Linux-source-structure group. The capable store search ^Linux-source request should list the latest piece structure packaged by Kali. Note that the source code contained in these groups doesn't contrast certainly and that dispersed by Linus Torvalds and the piece developers4;like all movements, Debian and Kali apply different patches, which may (or may not) find their way into the upstream type of Linux. These changes fuse backports of fixes/features/drivers from additional exceptional part frames, new features not yet (by and large) met in the upstream

Linux tree, and a portion of the time even Debian or Kali unequivocal changes.

The subsequent stage comprises of arranging the part as indicated by your needs. The careful method relies upon the objectives. The piece construct relies upon a portion arrangement document. By and large, you will no doubt keep as close as conceivable to that proposed by Kali, which, similar to all Linux dispersions, is introduced in the/boot catalogue. For this situation, as opposed to reconfiguring everything without any preparation, it is adequate to make a duplicate of the/boot/config-variant record. (The rendition ought to be equivalent to that form of the bit right now utilized, which can be found with the uname - r order.) place the duplicate into a config document in the index containing the part sources.

$ cp/boot/config-4.9.0-kali1-amd64 ~/piece/linux-source-4.9/.config

Then again, since the part gives default setups in curve/curve/configs/*_defconfig, you can set up your chose arrangement with a direction like make x86_64_defconfig (on account of a 64-piece pc) or make i386_defconfig (on account of a 32-piece pc). except if you have to change the setup, you can stop here and jump to segment 9.2.4, "Accumulating and Building the package" [page 235]. In the event that you have to make changes or in the event that you choose to reconfigure everything without any preparation, you should set aside the effort to design your portion. There are different devoted interfaces in the piece source registry that can be utilized by calling the make target direction, where target is one of the qualities portrayed underneath. Make menu config orders and dispatches a book mode piece design interface (this is the place the libncurses5-dev bundle is required), which permits exploring the numerous accessible portion alternatives in a various levelled structure. Squeezing the 4QBDF key changes the estimation of the chose choice, and &oUFS approves the catch chose at the base of the screen; Select comes back to the chose sub-menu; exit shuts the present screen and moves back up in the pecking order; Help will show progressively point by point data on the job of the chose choice. The bolt keys permit moving inside the rundown of alternatives and catches. To leave the setup program, pick exit from the fundamental menu. The program at that point offers to spare the progressions that you have made; acknowledge whether you are happy with your decisions. Different interfaces have comparable highlights however they work inside progressively current graphical interfaces, for example, make xconfig, which utilizes a Qt graphical interface, and make g config, which utilizes GTK+. The previous requires libqt4-dev, while the last relies upon libglade2-dev and libgtk2.0-dev. When the piece arrangement is prepared, a straightforward make deb-pkg will produce up to five Debian bundles in standard .deb position: Linux-picture rendition, which contains the part picture and the related modules; Linux-headers-variant, which contains the header records required to construct outer modules; Linux-firmware-picture adaptation, which contains the firmware documents required by certain drivers (this bundle may be missing when you work from the portion sources gave by Debian or Kali); Linux-picture form dbg, which contains the investigating images for the bit picture and its modules; and Linux-libc-dev, which contains headers important to some client space libraries like GNU's c library (glibc). The form is characterized by the connection of the upstream form (as characterized by the bundle rendition. It reuses a similar form string with an affixed update that is consistently augmented (and put away in .adaptation), aside from in the event that you abrogate it with the earth variable.

To really utilize the fabricated bit, the main advance left is to introduce the necessary bundles with dpkg - I file.deb. The "Linux-picture" bundle is required; you just need to introduce the "linux-headers" bundle in the event that you have some outside bit modules to manufacture, which is the situation on the off chance that you have a few, "*-dkms" bundles introduced (check with dpkg - l "*-dkms" | grep ^ii). Different bundles are commonly not required (Unless you know why you need them!).

Kali Linux has a huge amount of usefulness and adaptability directly out of the crate. When Kali is introduced, you can play out a wide range of stunning accomplishments with a little direction, innovativeness, persistence, and practice. Be that as it may, you can likewise redo a Kali assemble so it contains explicit documents or bundles (to scale up or downsize execution and includes) and can play out specific capacities consequently. For instance, the Kali ISo of Doom5 and the Kali evil Wireless Access point6 are both magnificent tasks that depend on an exceptionally assembled execution of Kali Linux. How about we investigate the way toward rolling a custom Kali Linux ISo picture. official Kali ISo pictures are worked with live-build7, which is a lot of contents that takes into consideration the total robotization and customization of all features of ISo picture creation. The live-form suite utilizes a whole index structure as contribution for its arrangement. We store this design and some related partner contents in a Git archive. We will utilize this archive as a reason for building modified pictures.

Summary

The Kali Linux venture started discreetly in 2012, when offensive Security concluded that they needed to supplant their respected Backtrack Linux venture, which was physically kept up, with something that could turn into a real Debian derivative3, complete with the entirety of the necessary foundation and improved bundling strategies. The choice was made to manufacture Kali over the Debian dissemination since it is notable for its quality, solidness, and wide choice of accessible programming. That is the reason I (Raphael) engaged in this task, as a Debian expert. The main discharge (form 1.0) happened one year later, in March 2013, and depended on Debian 7 "Wheezy", Debian's steady conveyance at the time. In that first year of advancement, we bundled many pen-testing-related applications and manufactured the framework. Despite the fact that the quantity of uses is noteworthy, the application list has been fastidiously curated, dropping applications that never again worked or that copied highlights effectively accessible in better projects. During the two years following form 1.0, Kali discharged numerous gradual updates, extending the scope of accessible applications and improving equipment support, on account of more current portion discharges. With some interest in constant mix, we guaranteed that immeasurably significant bundles were kept in an installable state and that tweaked live pictures (a sign of the dissemination) could generally be made. In 2015, when Debian 8 "Jessie" turned out, we attempted to rebase Kali Linux over it. While Kali Linux 1.x stayed away from the GNoMe Shell (depending on GNoMe Fallback rather), in this rendition we chose to grasp and upgrade it: we added some GNoMe Shell expansions to procure missing highlights, most eminently the Applications menu. The consequence of that work became Kali Linux 2.0, distributed in August 2015.

In parallel, we expanded our endeavours to guarantee that Kali Linux consistently has the most recent variant of all pen-testing applications. Sadly, that objective was a piece inconsistent with the utilization of Debian Stable as a base for the conveyance, since it expected us to backport numerous bundles. This is because of the way that Debian Stable puts a need on the solidness of the product, frequently causing a long postponement from the arrival of an upstream update to when it is coordinated into the dispersion. Given our interest in constant joining, it was a serious characteristic move to rebase Kali Linux over Debian Testing with the goal that we could profit by the most recent adaptation of all Debian bundles when they were accessible. Debian Testing has a considerably more forceful update cycle, which is progressively perfect with the way of thinking of Kali Linux. This is, fundamentally, the idea of Kali Rolling. While the moving dispersion has been accessible for a long time, Kali 2016.1 was the main discharge to authoritatively grasp the moving idea of that circulation: when you introduce the most recent Kali discharge, your framework really tracks the Kali Rolling conveyance and each and every day you get new updates. Before, Kali discharges were previews of the fundamental Debian dispersion with Kali-explicit bundles infused into it. A moving dispersion has numerous advantages yet it additionally accompanies various difficulties, both for those of us who are building the dissemination and for the clients who need to adapt to an endless progression of updates and once in a while in reverse incongruent changes. This book intends to give you the information required to manage all that you may experience while dealing with your Kali Linux establishment.

The Kali Linux dispersion depends on Debian Testing9. In this manner, a large portion of the bundles accessible in Kali Linux come directly from this Debian storehouse. While Kali Linux depends vigorously on Debian, it is additionally completely autonomous as in we have our own framework and hold the opportunity to roll out any improvements we need.

on the Debian side, the supporters are working each day on refreshing bundles and transferring them to the Debian Unstable appropriation. From that point, bundles move to the Debian Testing appropriation once the most inconvenient bugs have been taken out. The relocation procedure additionally guarantees that no conditions are broken in Debian Testing. The objective is that Testing is consistently in a usable (or even releasable!) state. Debian Testing's objectives adjust very well to those of Kali Linux so we picked it as the base. To include the Kali-explicit bundles in the dispersion, we pursue a two-advance procedure. To start with, we take Debian Testing and power infuse our own Kali bundles (situated in our kali-dev-just archive) to assemble the kali-dev vault. This storehouse will part from time to time: for example, our Kali-explicit bundles probably won't be installable until they have been recompiled against more up to date libraries. In different circumstances, bundles that we have forked may likewise must be refreshed, either to become installable once more, or to fix the install ability of another bundle that relies upon a more up to date form of the forked bundle. Regardless, kali-dev isn't for end-clients. kali-moving is the dissemination that Kali Linux clients are relied upon to follow and is worked out of kali-dev similarly that Debian Testing is worked out of Debian Unstable. Bundles relocate just when all conditions can be fulfilled in the objective dissemination.

As a plan choice, we attempt to limit the quantity of forked bundles however much as could reasonably be expected. Be that as it may, so as to execute a portion of Kali's one of a kind highlights, a few changes must be made. To restrict the effect of these changes, we endeavour to send them upstream, either by incorporating the component legitimately, or by including the necessary snares so it is clear to empower the ideal highlights moving along without any more altering the upstream bundles themselves. The Kali package Tracker10 causes us to monitor our disparity with Debian. Whenever, we can look into which bundle has been forked and whether it is in a state of harmony with Debian, or if an update is required. every one of our bundles are kept up in Git reposiToRies11 facilitating a Debian branch and a Kali branch one next to the other. on account of this, refreshing a forked bundle is a straightforward two-advance procedure: update the Debian branch and afterward blend it into the Kali branch. While the quantity of forked bundles in Kali is generally low, the quantity of extra bundles is fairly high: in April 2017 there were just about 400. The vast majority of these bundles are free programming conforming to the Debian Free Software Guidelines12 and our definitive objective is keep up those bundles inside Debian at whatever point conceivable. That is the reason we endeavour to consent to the Debian policy13 and to pursue the great bundling rehearses utilized in Debian. Shockingly, there are likewise a significant number special cases where legitimate bundling was about difficult to make. Because of time being rare, scarcely any bundles have been pushed to Debian.

While Kali's centre can be immediately outlined as "infiltration testing and security reviewing", there are a wide range of assignments required behind those exercises. Kali Linux is worked as a structure, since it incorporates numerous devices covering altogether different use cases (however they may surely be utilized in blend during an infiltration test). For instance, Kali Linux can be utilized on different kinds of pcs: clearly on the pcs of infiltration analysers, yet additionally on servers of framework managers wishing to screen their system, on the workstations of measurable experts, and all the more startlingly, on stealthy implanted gadgets, normally with ARM cpUs, that can be dropped in the scope of a remote system or connected the pc of target clients. Many ARM gadgets are additionally immaculate assault machines because of their little structure factors and low power necessities. Kali Linux can likewise be sent in the cloud to rapidly assemble a ranch of secret key breaking machines and on cell phones and tablets to take into consideration really versatile entrance testing. In any case, that isn't all; entrance analysers additionally need servers: to utilize joint effort programming inside a group of pen-analysers, to set up a web server for use in phishing efforts, to run powerlessness checking instruments, and other related exercises. When you have booted Kali, you will rapidly find that Kali Linux's primary menu is sorted out by topic over the different sort of errands and exercises that are pertinent for pen-analysers and other data security experts.

Kali Linux is a Linux appropriation that contains its very own assortment of many programming apparatuses explicitly customized for their objective clients—entrance analysers and other security experts. It additionally accompanies an establishment program to totally arrangement Kali Linux as the fundamental working framework on any pc.

Kali Linux is worked by entrance analysers for infiltration analysers however we comprehend that not every person will concur with our plan choices or selection of apparatuses to incorporate of course. considering this, we generally guarantee that Kali Linux is anything but difficult to tweak dependent on your own needs and inclinations. To this end, we distribute the live-form setup used to manufacture the official Kali pictures so you can modify it just as you would prefer. It is anything but difficult to begin from this distributed design and execute different changes dependent on your needs because of the adaptability of live-form. Live-form incorporates numerous highlights to alter the introduced framework, introduce beneficial records, introduce extra bundles, run self-assertive directions, and change the qualities pre-seeded to deb conf.
clients of a security dispersion legitimately need to realize that it very well may be trusted and that it has been created on display, enabling anybody to investigate the source code. Kali Linux is created by a little group of learned engineers working straightforwardly and following the best security rehearses: they transfer marked source bundles, which are then based on committed form daemons. The bundles are then check summed and conveyed as a major aspect of a marked storehouse.

References

1. _"official Kali Linux Releases". Recovered 2019-11-26._

2. _^ "official Kali Linux Releases". Recovered 2019-09-03._

3. _^ Jump up to:a b NesToR, Marius. "Kali Linux ethical Hacking oS Switches to Xfce Desktop, Gets New Look and Feel". softpedia. Recovered 2019-11-29._

4. _^ "Kali Linux 1.0 survey". LinuxBSDos.com. 2013-03-14. Recovered 2019-11-26._

5. _^ Simionato, Lorenzo (2007-04-24). "Survey: BackTrack 2 security live cD". Linux.com. Recovered 2019-04-10._

6. _^ Barr, Joe. "Test your condition's security with BackTrack". Linux.com. Recovered 2019-04-10._

7. _^ "BackTrack 4 - Hacking in abundance". Dedoimedo.com. 2009-05-15. Recovered 2019-04-10._

8. _^ "BackTrack 5 R3 survey". LinuxBSDos.com. 2012-08-17. Recovered 2019-04-10._

9. _^ Watson, J.A. (2014-05-28). "Hands-on with Kali Linux 1.0.7". ZDNet.com. Recovered 2019-04-10._

10. _^ "Kali Linux 1.0.7 survey". LinuxBSDos.com. 2014-05-30. Recovered 2019-04-10._

11. _^ "Kali Linux survey". Dedoimedo.com. 2014-12-15. Recovered 2019-04-10._

12. _^ Watson, J.A. (2016-01-22). "Hands-on with Kali Linux Rolling". ZDNet.com. Recovered 2019-04-10._

13. _^ Smith, Jesse (2016-04-25). "Kali Linux 2016.1". DistroWatch Weekly. No. 658. Recovered 2019-04-10._

14. _^ Jump up to:a b "Kali Linux penetration Testing Tools". tools.kali.org. Recovered 2019-04-10._

15. _^ Jump up to:a b "Kali Linux lands as big business prepared form of BackTrack". The H. 2013-03-13. Recovered 2019-04-10._

16. _^ "Kali Linux Metapackages". Hostile Security. Recovered 2019-04-10._

17. _^ "The Birth of Kali Linux". Hostile Security. 2012-12-12. Recovered 2019-04-10._

18. ^ Jump up to:a b orin, Andy (2014-12-03). "Behind the App: The SToRy of Kali Linux". Lifehacker. Recovered 2019-04-10. Mati Aharoni: one of our objectives with Kali is to give pictures of the working framework for a wide range of extraordinary equipment— principally ARM based. This incorporates everything from Raspberry pi's to tablets, to Android TV gadgets, with each bit of equipment having some one of a kind property.

19. ^ "Kali's Relationship With Debian". Kali Linux. 2013-03-11. Recovered 2019-04-10.

20. ^ "A Bit of HisToRy". kali.training. Recovered 2019-04-10.

21. ^ "Kali Linux Hard Disk Install". Kali Linux official Documentation. Recovered 2019-04-10.

22. ^ pauli, Darren (2013-03-13). "BackTrack successor Kali Linux propelled". Sc Magazine. Recovered 2019-04-10.

23. ^ "04. Kali Linux on ARM". Recovered 2019-09-04.

24. ^ muts (2018-03-05). "Kali Linux in the Windows App SToRe". Kali Linux. Recovered 2019-04-10.

25. ^ Jump up to:a b "Kali Linux NetHunter for Nexus and oneplus". Recovered 2019-04-10.

26. ^ "Kali Linux Forensics Mode". Recovered 2019-04-10.

outer connections

- Kali 2019.4 – 26th November, 2019 – The fourth 2019 Kali Rolling discharge. piece 5.3.9, XFce 4.14.1

- Kali 2019.3 – second September, 2019 – The third 2019 Kali Rolling discharge. piece 5.2.9, GNoMe 3.30.2

- Kali 2019.2 – 21st May, 2019 – The second 2019 Kali Rolling discharge. piece 4.19.28, GNoMe 3.30.2

- Kali 2019.1a – fourth March, 2019 – Minor BugFix discharge (VMware Installer).

- Kali 2019.1 – eighteenth February, 2019 – The initial 2019 Kali Rolling discharge. piece 4.19.13, GNoMe 3.30.2

- Kali 2018.4 – 29th october, 2018 – The fourth 2018 Kali Rolling discharge. piece 4.18.0, GNoMe 3.30.1

- Kali 2018.3 – 27th August, 2018 – The third 2018 Kali Rolling discharge. piece 4.17.0, GNoMe 3.28.2

- Kali 2018.2 – 30th April, 2018 – The second 2018 Kali Rolling discharge. piece 4.15.0, GNoMe 3.28.0

- Kali 2018.1 – sixth February, 2018 – The initial 2018 Kali Rolling discharge. piece 4.14.12, GNoMe 3.26.2

- _Kali 2017.3 – 21st November, 2017 – The third 2017 Kali Rolling discharge. piece 4.13, GNoMe 3.26_
- _Kali 2017.2 – twentieth September, 2017 – The second 2017 Kali Rolling discharge. piece 4.12, GNoMe 3.25._
- _Kali 2017.1 – 25th April, 2017 – The initial 2017 Kali Rolling discharge. Bit 4.9, GNoMe 3.22._
- _Kali 2016.2 – 31st August, 2016 – The subsequent Kali Rolling discharge. Bit 4.6, GNoMe 3.20.2._
- _Kali 2016.1 – 21st January, 2016 – The main Kali Rolling discharge. piece 4.3, GNoMe 3.18._
- _Kali 2.0 – eleventh August, 2015 – Major discharge, "safi", presently a moving conveyance, major UI changes._
- _Kali 1.1.0a – thirteenth March, 2015 – No ballyhoo discharge fixing portion ABI irregularities in the installers._
- _Kali 1.1.0 – ninth Febuary, 2015 – First spot discharge in 2 years. New portion, new instruments and updates._
- _Kali 1.0.9a – sixth october, 2014 – Security BugFix discharge covering shellshock and Debian able vulnerabilities._
- _Kali 1.0.9 – 25th August, 2014 – BugFix discharge including installer and a lot of hardware updates and bundle fixes._
- _Kali 1.0.8 – 22nd July, 2014 – eFI Support for our "full" ISos and a lot of hardware updates and bundle fixes._
- _Kali 1.0.7 – 27th May, 2014 – Kernel 3.14, device refreshes, bundle fixes, Kali Live encrypted USB persistence._
- _Kali 1.0.6 – ninth January, 2014 – Kernel 3.12, cryptsetup nuke choice, Amazon AMI, ARM fabricate contents._
- _Kali 1.0.5 – fifth September, 2013 – BugFix rollup. LVM encrypted introduces, Software Defined Radio (SDR) apparatuses._
- _Kali 1.0.4 – 25th July, 2013 – BugFix rollup. Infiltration testing apparatus increases and updates._
- _Kali 1.0.3 – 26th April, 2013 – BugFix rollup. New openness highlights. Included live Desktop installer._
- _Kali 1.0.2 – 27th March, 2013 – Minor BugFix discharge and update move up._
- _Kali 1.0.1 – fourteenth March, 2013 – Minor BugFix discharge (USB Keyboard)._
- _Kali 1.0.0 – thirteenth March, 2013 – Initial discharge, "moto"._

- *Kali 2017.2 – twentieth September, 2017 – The second 2017 Kali Rolling discharge. Bit 4.12, GNoMe 3.25.*
- *Kali 2017.1 – 25th April, 2017 – The initial 2017 Kali Rolling discharge. Bit 4.9, GNoMe 3.22.*
- *Kali 2016.2 – 31st August, 2016 – The subsequent Kali Rolling discharge. Bit 4.6, GNoMe 3.20.2.*
- *Kali 2016.1 – 21st January, 2016 – The principal Kali Rolling discharge. Bit 4.3, GNoMe 3.18.*
- *Kali 2.0 – eleventh August, 2015 – Major discharge, "safi", presently a moving circulation, major UI changes.*
- *Kali 1.1.0a – thirteenth March, 2015 – No display discharge fixing portion ABI irregularities in the installers.*
- *Kali 1.1.0 – ninth Febuary, 2015 – First speck discharge in 2 years. New portion, new devices and updates.*
- *Kali 1.0.9a – sixth october, 2014 – Security BugFix discharge covering shellshock and Debian adept vulnerabilities.*
- *Kali 1.0.9 – 25th August, 2014 – BugFix discharge including installer and a lot of hardware updates and bundle fixes.*
- *Kali 1.0.8 – 22nd July, 2014 – eFI Support for our "full" ISos and a lot of hardware updates and bundle fixes.*
- *Kali 1.0.7 – 27th May, 2014 – Kernel 3.14, apparatus refreshes, bundle fixes, Kali Live encrypted USB persistence.*
- *Kali 1.0.6 – ninth January, 2014 – Kernel 3.12, cryptsetup nuke choice, Amazon AMI, ARM manufacture contents.*
- *Kali 1.0.5 – fifth September, 2013 – BugFix rollup. LVM encrypted introduces, Software Defined Radio (SDR) instruments.*
- *Kali 2017.2 – twentieth September, 2017 – The second 2017 Kali Rolling discharge. Bit 4.12, GNoMe 3.25.*
- *Kali 2017.1 – 25th April, 2017 – The initial 2017 Kali Rolling discharge. Bit 4.9, GNoMe 3.22.*
- *Kali 2016.2 – 31st August, 2016 – The subsequent Kali Rolling discharge. Bit 4.6, GNoMe 3.20.2.*
- *Kali 2016.1 – 21st January, 2016 – The principal Kali Rolling discharge. portion 4.3, GNoMe 3.18.*
- *Kali 2.0 – eleventh August, 2015 – Major discharge, "safi", presently a moving dispersion, major UI changes.*

- *Kali 1.1.0a – thirteenth March, 2015 – No pomp discharge fixing portion ABI irregularities in the installers.*
- *Kali 1.1.0 – ninth Febuary, 2015 – First spot discharge in 2 years. New portion, new apparatuses and refreshes.*
- *Kali 1.0.9a – sixth october, 2014 – Security BugFix discharge covering shellshock and Debian well-suited vulnerabilities.*
- *Kali 1.0.9 – 25th August, 2014 – BugFix discharge including installer and a lot of hardware updates and bundle fixes.*
- *Kali 1.0.8 – 22nd July, 2014 – eFI Support for our "full" ISos and a lot of hardware updates and bundle fixes.*
- *Kali 1.0.7 – 27th May, 2014 – Kernel 3.14, instrument refreshes, bundle fixes, Kali Live encrypted USB persistence.*
- *Kali 1.0.6 – ninth January, 2014 – Kernel 3.12, cryptsetup nuke choice, Amazon AMI, ARM manufacture contents.*
- *Kali 1.0.5 – fifth September, 2013 – BugFix rollup. LVM encrypted introduces, Software Defined Radio (SDR) devices.*
- *Kali 2017.2 – twentieth September, 2017 – The second 2017 Kali Rolling discharge. part 4.12, GNoMe 3.25.*
- *Kali 2017.1 – 25th April, 2017 – The initial 2017 Kali Rolling discharge. part 4.9, GNoMe 3.22.*
- *Kali 2016.2 – 31st August, 2016 – The subsequent Kali Rolling discharge. part 4.6, GNoMe 3.20.2.*
- *Kali 2016.1 – 21st January, 2016 – The primary Kali Rolling discharge. part 4.3, GNoMe 3.18.*
- *Kali 2.0 – eleventh August, 2015 – Major discharge, "safi", presently a moving dispersion, major UI changes.*
- *Kali 1.1.0a – thirteenth March, 2015 – No show discharge fixing bit ABI irregularities in the installers.*
- *Kali 1.1.0 – ninth Febuary, 2015 – First speck discharge in 2 years. New bit, new instruments and updates.*
- *Kali 1.0.9a – sixth october, 2014 – Security BugFix discharge covering shellshock and Debian able vulnerabilities.*
- *Kali 1.0.9 – 25th August, 2014 – BugFix discharge including installer and a lot of hardware updates and bundle fixes.*
- *Kali 1.0.8 – 22nd July, 2014 – eFI Support for our "full" ISos and a lot of hardware updates and bundle fixes.*

- *Kali 1.0.7 – 27th May, 2014 – Kernel 3.14, device refreshes, bundle fixes, Kali Live encrypted USB persistence.*
- *Kali 1.0.6 – ninth January, 2014 – Kernel 3.12, cryptsetup nuke choice, Amazon AMI, ARM assemble contents.*
- *Kali 1.0.5 – fifth September, 2013 – BugFix rollup. LVM encrypted*

CPSIA information can be obtained
at www.ICGtesting.com
Printed in the USA
LVHW051811060223
738796LV00012B/1321